elwha

elwha
A RIVER REBORN

LYNDA V. MAPES
PHOTOGRAPHY BY STEVE RINGMAN
CO-PUBLISHED WITH THE SEATTLE TIMES

THE MOUNTAINEERS BOOKS

THE MOUNTAINEERS BOOKS
is the nonprofit publishing arm of The Mountaineers, an organization founded in 1906 and
dedicated to the exploration, preservation, and enjoyment of outdoor and wilderness areas.

1001 SW Klickitat Way, Suite 201, Seattle, WA 98134

Distributed in the United Kingdom by Cordee, www.cordee.co.uk
Manufactured in China

Copy Editor: Kris Fulsaas
Cover, Book Design, and Layout: Heidi Smets Graphic Design
Cartographer: Ani Rucki
All photographs by Steve Ringman unless otherwise noted.

Cover photograph: (Top left) *Moss brings new life to the former Lake Aldwell;* (Right) *Elwha Hatchery fish spawn
controversy;* (Bottom) *Elwha Dam, built in 1910, blocked Elwha salmon and steelhead from their native waters for one
hundred years.*

Frontispiece: *Elwha Dam, built beginning in 1910 without fish passage, blocked migration to 90 percent of the river's
spawning grounds for salmon and steelhead.*

Page 176: *An eagle surveys the transformation underway as sand released with the removal of Elwha Dam in March,
2012 reaches the beach in June, softening an eroded stretch of shoreline. Dam removal is sparking dramatic changes,
from the mountains to the sea.*

Library of Congress Cataloging-in-Publication data on file

ISBN (paperback): 978-1-59485-734-8
ISBN (ebook): 978-1-59485-735-5

Cover and interior printed on FSC-certified papers

TO MY FATHER, LYNN C. MAPES, WITH LOVE AND GRATITUDE
—L.V.M.

TO MY FATHER, ROBERT RINGMAN, WHO NURTURED MY LOVE OF PHOTOGRAPHY
—S.R.

The largest dam removal ever undertaken anywhere, the Elwha project attracted scientists from around the country to gather baseline data against which to measure change during and after dam removal. This snorkeler is surveying fish populations.

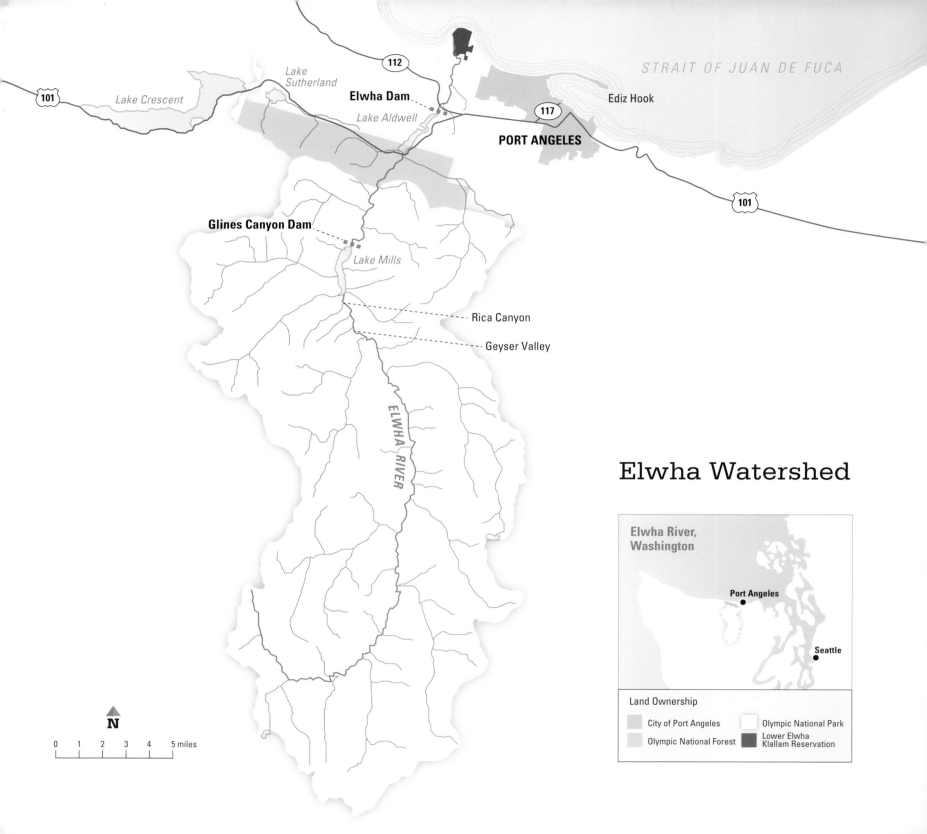

STRAIT OF JUAN DE FUCA

Ediz Hook

Lake Crescent

Lake Sutherland

Elwha Dam

Lake Aldwell

PORT ANGELES

Glines Canyon Dam

Lake Mills

Rica Canyon

Geyser Valley

ELWHA RIVER

112

101

117

101

Elwha Watershed

Elwha River, Washington

Port Angeles

Seattle

Land Ownership

City of Port Angeles

Olympic National Forest

Olympic National Park

Lower Elwha Klallam Reservation

N

0   1   2   3   4   5 miles

PREFACE

On the front steps of our house in Seattle, where most people have pots of geraniums, I keep several hunks of the Elwha Dam—not as a trophy, but as a reminder. Returning in March 2012 to the site where the Elwha Dam used to be was a bit of a shock. The dam was so completely gone, it was hard to imagine it had ever been there at all. The hill where it used to squat was scraped bare, the bald ground—worked over by heavy equipment—not yet home to a blade of grass, not even a weed. As I walked it, the deep mud pulling at my boots, pieces of the past were everywhere: an old wooden wagon wheel, rusty pieces of steel cable, hunks of ceramic insulators from the powerlines. The future here had yet to take root. But the river was already back—roaring through its native channel, plugged by the dam for a century, as if nothing had ever been amiss. As of about 5:00 PM on March 9, 2012, the Elwha Dam was history.

In a construction trailer not far from where the dam used to be, I talked with the project manager on the deconstruction job about how the dam had so easily toppled, its crumbling concrete one reason the dam had always leaked. As he talked, I recognized the American flag that used to fly over one of the dams tacked on the trailer wall opposite his desk. With its tattered edge, it had the feel of a trophy, taken in war.

And war it was. For more than twenty-five years, conservationists, tribal leaders, Washington's congressional delegation, industrialists, lawyers and lobbyists, and local, state, and federal policy makers slugged it out over the Elwha Dam and Glines Canyon Dam, 8.6 miles upriver. They fought over the cost of taking them out, how to do it, whether to do it, and who should pay. Whether it would work. Who should be compensated, and how. In the end, freeing the Elwha cost three times as much, and took ten times longer to get underway, than anyone originally forecast. Nearly twenty years passed from the time Congress in 1992 passed Public Law No. 102-495, the Elwha River Ecosystem and Fisheries Restoration Act, until the first excavator bucket, painted gold for the occasion, smashed into the concrete in a ceremony at the Elwha Dam on September 17, 2011.

Tearing down the Elwha Dam, 108 feet tall, and the Glines Canyon Dam, 210 feet tall, would be the largest dam removal project ever in the world, opening more than 70 miles of spawning habitat to steelhead and all five species of Pacific salmon (chinook, chum, coho, pink, and sockeye). With more than 83 percent of its 321-square-mile watershed still pristine and permanently protected in Olympic National Park in the northwest corner of Washington State, the $325 million federal project offered a rare chance to restore a legendary wilderness river valley.

After the shock of seeing used-to-be-Elwha, I headed to visit what was left of Glines, where the drama of demolition was still unfolding. From the walkway perched just aside the dam, I looked down more than 60 feet into the hole the operator of a giant hydraulic hammer chisel had bashed in the face of the dam, chipping it down chunk by chunk. As he lowered the chisel for another blow, it disappeared from view under the water cascading through the widening hole, pouring into the canyon below and throwing a double rainbow of spray. In about another year, that dam would be gone too.

As the reservoirs drained down about 1.5 feet a day, the river already was cutting through deltas of sediment backed up for decades behind the dams, creating badlands of sculpted, terraced fine material. Milky with sediment, the river carved soft cliffs where entire hunks had fallen away at once, calving into the water and leaving the cliff sides smooth. Where the lowering water levels of the reservoir left their mark in ripples and ridges, the cliff sides were gray and wrinkled as elephant skin. On the flats, tiny raccoon footprints showed animals even now were exploring the new landscape. It was easy hiking, soft as a sandy beach. Along the river, a ghost forest graveyard offered hints of the grandeur that had been: gigantic cedar stumps wider than a king-size bed studded the flats. They were all that remained of the trees logged off before the gates of the dam were shut and the forest turned into a lake.

On the sediment badlands above the river, the pioneers of what might one day be a forest again were already in the ground: native plants raised from seeds gathered in the Elwha valley, part of an unprecedented replanting effort by the National Park Service to stabilize the more than 800 acres that eventually will be exposed in the former lake beds. As I walked the emerging landscape in the fierce spring wind, it was hard to imagine these tender plant starts surviving in the gray grit. In fine silt, 5 feet and more thick that would bake hard as a brick in the summer sun, in sand drifting and blowing, with no soil or practical way to add compost or provide irrigation on so large an area—what could live here? Of some 350 Douglas fir seedlings planted on this terrace in the winter of 2011–12, more than sixty were already dead by May.

But nature is, if anything, resilient; all around me, the music and motion of the river was revived where it had been silenced and stilled in reservoirs just weeks ago. And somewhere, out there in the North Pacific, were the salmon and steelhead whose genetic code still urges them home to this river. Even after all these years, a storied run of fall chinook, which back before the dams could grow as large as a hundred pounds, still return to what's left of their spawning ground in the lower river, swimming as far upstream as possible before being stopped at the lower dam, built without fish passage. Scientists think once both dams are out, those fish, still genetically distinct from other Puget Sound chinook, will one day thrash up to the very feet of Mount Olympus. Food indeed fit for the gods—but also for a whole suite of life, from shrews to river otters, mink, bears, eagles, insects, and more, sustaining an entire watershed starving for the feast of fish from the sea.

Renewal of the Elwha ecosystem has broader implications, too. The Lower Elwha Klallam Tribe, the first people of the watershed, lost the most when the dams went in and stand to reap some of the most profound gains as the dams come out. In the return of wholeness to the landscape, tribal members say, is the return of wholeness to the people. Not only for the tribe, but also for the rest of us.

Beginning in the summer of 2010, *The Seattle Times* sent staff photographer Steve Ringman and me out to begin a long-term exploration of the Elwha River and its historic transformation. Our work took us to the Lower Elwha Klallam Tribe's reservation near the river's mouth near Port Angeles, where we heard stories of loss and of renewal. It took us into the raucous main stem of the river and into the lush, secret worlds of its unnamed floodplain channels. We camped in fern-padded elk flats amid the big-leaf maple forests just up from the river's gravel bars. We watched fish regurgitate their meals as scientists investigated

Anna Torrance, right, and Heidi Hugunin, fish technicians for the National Park Service, take stock of the river's channel prior to the beginning of dam removal in 2011.

their diet. We barged right into the river, fighting its attempts to topple us over, carefully placing one foot after another on slime-slick, wet rocks. We ran the river's foaming green slide in rafts, the wind spanking the collars of our life jackets against our necks. We shook hands with the man running the Elwha Dam single-handedly, as the river rattled the powerhouse and spun generators roaring with its energy. We watched elk vanish into alder terraces and salmon bullet upriver, called by the first fall rains. We endured borrowed waders that turned out to be less than watertight and shivered in rafts spun backward down the Elwha, ricocheting between boulders.

The scientists helped. From five agencies and the Lower Elwha Klallam Tribe, they had teamed up for more than ten years, doing baseline studies of the Elwha ecosystem. During the fieldwork seasons of 2010 and 2011, they let us join their explorations as they probed the Elwha watershed prior to dam removal. To a man and to a woman, and nearly to a fault, they watched out for us as we crossed the river that snarled high around our legs, shared their coffeepot in the morning and their campfire at night. We came along as they measured the riverbed cobble and probed the depths of its pools. We watched them plant set nets, pull beach seines, and zap back eddies with a backpack electrofisher. We saw them trap, count, weigh, sex, and tag returning adult salmon muscling into a temporary weir, built right across the Elwha. We went along as they baited live traps with dripping, stinky salmon heads to entice river otters. Watched them string mist nets across the river to (briefly) capture and sample songbirds. Trailed them as they snuck in camouflage through hip-high ferns, toting a gun loaded with 6-inch-long darts packed with sleeping potion, tracking elk to radio-collar.

We learned why it took nearly twenty years to get the dams out after the passage of the Elwha restoration act—and the cost to taxpayers of finally cutting a deal that would stick. We came to understand the triumph that building the dams had been for the industrialists and boosters of Port Angeles, as well as their devastating effects on the Lower Elwha Klallam Tribe. We witnessed the tribe's perseverance that in the end answered their ancestors' prayers. And as we worked, Steve and I encountered many unsettled questions about the future. For this is a book about a place where enormous change has played out—and a lot more is coming.

■ ■ ■

There's a unique resonance in the telling and the publishing of this story by two Northwest institutions: *The Seattle Times*, founded in Seattle in 1896 by the Blethen family, which still owns and runs the newspaper, and the Mountaineers, founded in Seattle in 1906, which continues to be one of the largest outdoor recreation organizations in the country. Both have been backing explorations of the Elwha since before the dams were built—and writing about it ever since.

When the Mountaineers embarked on what was to become its annual summer outing in the Olympics in 1907, it was front-page news in the August 3 afternoon edition of the *Seattle Daily Times*. "Fifty who started July 24 report pleasant time, dwelling in sylvan groves, and eating six-course dinner," says the subhead on the story, recounting the 65-mile hike in the Elwha Basin, including an ascent of Mount Olympus. A photo caption notes, "The feminine element was well represented."

Of course. And of course the hike was front-page news: Seattle has a long-running love affair with the Olympics. It's

A yodeler routs climbers from their tents on a Mountaineers outing by the Elwha in September, 1951. The outings were often front page news in *The Seattle Times* for readers fascinated with the allure of the Olympic backcountry. (*Seattle Times,* 1951)

the wilderness beckoning in plain sight from downtown, the peaks of the Brothers gleaming with fresh snow seemingly just an arm's reach from neighborhoods all over Seattle. The mountains entice, ridge upon ridge receding into purple- and blue-shadowed distance.

As the restless, boundary-testing nineteenth century drew to a close, the Olympics remained a target ripe for exploration.

No crossing of the Olympics by the newcomers to this land had yet been documented, and the mountains, in their cloud-veiled mystery, teased and beckoned. "The mountains seem to rise from the edge of the water . . . in steep ascent to the line of perpetual snow, as though nature has designed to shut up this spot for her safe retreat forever," wrote Eugene Semple, governor of Washington Territory in his report to the Department of the Interior in 1888. "Here she is entrenched behind frowning walls of basalt, in front of which is Hood's canal, deep, silent, dark, and eternal, constituting the moat. Down in its unfathomable water lurks the giant squid, and on its shores the cinnamon bear and the cougar wander in the solitude of the primeval forest. It is a land of mystery, awe-inspiring in its mighty constituents and wonder-making in its unknown expanse of canyon and ridge."

The Elwha will never again be the Eden it was, and it's no longer an unmapped wilderness. But what could we learn of this place after all these years and the changes time has wrought? What could it mean to restore a river ecosystem, all the way from the mountains to the sea? How did a region synonymous with hydropower become the world's biggest dam-busting pioneer? How would this place, with its human and natural history so intimately connected, be transformed as it was taken apart and put back together?

Off we went to find out.

—Lynda V. Mapes
Seattle, Washington
April 2012

Jeff Duda, research ecologist with the USGS Western Fisheries Research Center in Seattle, sets up a seine in the Elwha to gather specimens for analysis.

ACKNOWLEDGMENTS

Many people helped with the creation of this book. I am deeply grateful to my colleague, Steve Ringman. His willingness to stay with the story paid off in the rich visual telling in the newspaper and online, and now in this book. I also am grateful to *Seattle Times* publisher Frank Blethen and editors Kathy Best, David Boardman, Suki Dardarian, Mark Higgins, Matt Kreamer, and Jim Simon, who supported years of beat reporting on the Elwha. *Seattle Times* photo editors Angela Gottschalk and Fred Nelson guided the photographic illustration of the Elwha story and supported Steve in establishing and sustaining his spectacular artistic engagement. I am grateful to Janet Kimball, project editor, for her patience, good questions, and eye for detail, and to Kate Rogers, editor in chief for the Mountaineers Books, for her enthusiastic support for this book. Evelyn Edens Ringman, new business development manager at *The Seattle Times*, made the many details of putting this book project together look easy, but I know it wasn't.

Many scientists shared their knowledge. Tim Abbe, Jim Adelman, David Allen, Jennifer Bountry, Sam Brenkman, Joshua Chenoweth, Amy Draut, Jeff Duda, Gordon Grant, Mike McHenry, John McMillan, Ian Miller, Sarah Morley, George Pess, Tim Randle, Andy Ritchie, Kim Sager-Fradkin, and Jonathan Warrick were particularly helpful. I am also grateful to Adeline Smith and the late Bea Charles, Mark Charles, Mel Elofson, Rachael Hagaman, and Jamie Valadez, of the Lower Elwha Klallam Tribe, as well as Frances Charles, tribal chairwoman. Orville Campbell, manager of the dams for many years; Noreen Frink, Thomas Aldwell's granddaughter; and Shawn Cantrell at Seattle Audubon, Joe Mentor, and David Ortman generously shared their knowledge and their archives. The research librarians at the University of Washington Libraries Special Collections and archivists at the Washington State Archives, as well as Kathy Monds, executive director of the Clallam County Historical Society and the society's researcher, Dona Cloud, were a wonderful help. I am grateful too for Marcy Woodruff's generous hospitality while I worked in Port Angeles and the assistance of many National Park Service staff, especially Barb Maynes and Brian Winter. Billy Cargo, Bob Williams, and Kevin Yancy, all of who worked at the dams, brought the human touch to those big machines.

Finally, I thank my friends and family for all their love and support.

The iconic image of Lake Mills glimmering in the high country of the Elwha is but a memory now. Removal of 210-foot high

1

TOO LONG TOO QUIET

We headed single file down the trail from the Whiskey Bend trailhead huffing under a mountain of gear. This was backcountry science, bushwhacking through willow whips and devil's club, in hidden landscapes probed best by an old-fashioned boot survey. The Elwha River would be our laboratory for the next few days as we shadowed a team of scientists from a host of different agencies led by George Pess, a supervisory research fish biologist at Seattle's National Oceanic and Atmospheric Administration's Northwest Fisheries Science Center.

The river and its surrounding forest are reunited as the Elwha returns to its native channel in March, 2012. With Elwha Dam gone, Lake Aldwell drained, revealing the forest cut before the river was drowned and silenced beneath the reservoir.

Pess turned out for fieldwork in the sweater his mother knit him in high school; his lunch was home-cooked stuffed peppers packed in a plastic container. His camping gear was Coleman, and his chocolate Milky Way. He set the tone for this work crew, whose motto in the field was "you are only as good as your data"—data gathered in a setting where the river makes the rules.

Here, simple techniques turned out to be the most efficient: snorkeling, walking, fishing, beach seining, hand counting. The tools were rudimentary—basically, whatever could be lugged into the backcountry: rulers, five-gallon plastic buckets, Global Positioning System devices, plastic food-storage containers, waterproof notebooks, pencils, sieves, sample bottles, fishing rods, drift nets. But while the tools were low-tech, the mission was ambitious: to study this river, looking back more than a decade before dam removal and, hopefully, for years to come beyond it.

One of the team's goals was to pilot simple research methods that worked in the backcountry and could later be repeated. No one method was perfect, and they all had their trade-offs. Working in a big system like the Elwha, science is the art of the possible. Nets break, and the river's current kicks like an irritable mule. In the Elwha—too big and wild much of the year to work in at all—field time is precious, and any results hard won through patient work.

The team was starting a field season of meticulous research to observe the river's baseline condition before the dams came out, from the lower 5 miles of the river to its middle reaches and all the way to its wilderness stretches in the upper river—Geyser Valley, Elkhorn, and higher. Everything needed documentation: the flow rate of the water, the size of the rocks, the

Elwha Dam was constructed just 5 miles from the mouth of the Elwha River without fish passage, blocking 93 percent of the spawning habitat for ocean-going fish in the Elwha watershed, including all five species of Pacific salmon and steelhead.

depths of the pools, the aquatic invertebrates in the water and the river bottom, and even in the bellies of the fish. Nothing was left to guesswork, as these scientists worked to discern the physical and biological characteristics of the river on the verge of dam removal.

We dumped everything on the maple flats above the Elwha River at Krause Bottom, in the upper reaches of the river's fast, green run through Olympic National Park in the northwest corner of Washington State. Struggling to keep up, we were amazed at the pace Pess set. Avoiding piles of elk pellets, we quickly set up our tents so we wouldn't have to deal with that

For a century, only landlocked fish such as rainbow trout were found in the Elwha above the dams. Elwha dam removal restores 70 miles of spawning habitat and is one of the best chances for large scale, permanent environmental restoration anywhere.

later, probably in the dark. Scrambling down the bank, we split into teams to work. I joined biologist John McMillan, also with NOAA's Northwest Fisheries Science Center, as he grabbed a rod to get some fish for his colleague Sarah Morley to help her figure out what the resident trout were eating. McMillan headed upriver to fish the cool, shady pools under the logjams. The son of Bill McMillan, a storied angler and conservationist, John is a native of Western Washington who has fished all his life. "I've spent fifteen years fishing 300 days a year; I have caught thousands of steelhead," McMillan said. "Now I've reached a point where the fish aren't doing well enough, and I don't even want to do it anymore."

He'd snorkeled many reaches of this river, surveying fish populations. Especially in the main channel, it can be a steep,

fast, dangerous run of a mountain river leaving little room for mistakes. "Kayakers love them," McMillan said of the Olympic Peninsula's mountain rivers. "Snorkelers fear them." Yet these snorkel surveys had given him a rare look at the Elwha's fish, a peek into the unseen world under the surface. "It's a beautiful world; the fingers of light reach down like in a cathedral," McMillan said. Up here in the backcountry, he also felt he was getting face time with fish that had never seen people. "They are friendly; they look at you unafraid, as if to say, 'You are not an otter.'"

A raven gronked deep in the forest, and the Elwha threw reflections of sunlight on the rocks as McMillan stood on a gravel bar, flicking a dry fly onto the river's surface. Cottonwoods towered over the willows scribbled at the water's edge; the sandbar we stood on was soft and already warmed by the morning sun. White moths fluttered like tiny handkerchiefs in the tangles of riverside plants. Even now the heat was building on this rare, perfect summer day, the iron-gray mists that swaddle the Elwha much of the year hardly imaginable. Skunked, McMillan switched gear to a nymph and scrabbled atop a silvered trunk in a towering battlement of logs impounding a pool off the river's main channel. Denied again, he knelt to fish a pool shaded by a log. A belted kingfisher clattered nearby, surely a good sign.

In just about another year, demolition would get underway on the Elwha and Glines Canyon dams that had choked this legendary wilderness river for a century. Dams this big, built at about 5 and 14 miles, respectively, from the river's mouth beginning in 1910, had never been taken down before. Especially in a setting like this, where 83 percent of the watershed was otherwise still prime habitat, permanently protected

With its elegant curve and simple lines, Glines Canyon Dam, built beginning in 1926, 8.6 miles upriver from Elwha Dam, was always the looker of the two. Together the dams produced enough electricity to power about 15,000 average homes.

Andy Ritchie, Elwha restoration project hydrologist for the National Park Service, examines bits of the native forest floor along the Elwha, exposed in March, 2011 by the erosive power of the river unleashed from Elwha Dam.

within a national park. It was a unique situation. "We don't have any examples where we've taken the foot off the neck where so much of the watershed is in pristine condition," McMillan said. He didn't doubt the salmon and steelhead would boom back. He was nine years old when Mount St. Helens erupted on May 18, 1980, plugging the Toutle River with ash. Yet the salmon survived that volcanic blast, recolonizing the river, just as they recolonized Puget Sound in its entirety after the retreat of the glaciers 10,000 years ago. By comparison, McMillan said, two dams didn't seem like much to get over. "Nature puts itself back together with the parts it has. How fast will they come back?" he asked of the Elwha's legendary fish runs. "Maybe in two generations? In ten? But these are the veins and arteries and capillaries of the system, where all the spawning happens."

Eagerly awaited are the Elwha fall chinook. The biggest salmon in Puget Sound, they were so vital, so integral, and so important to this place that in Chinook jargon, their name *tyee* is synonymous with chiefly status. But Elwha River restoration is so much more than a fish story. Taking the dams out is about rebuilding the whole house of *tyee*.

With the dams gone, all of the wheels within wheels of the Elwha's interconnected lives and processes—from nutrient cycling to the distribution of gravel and big wood, to the shaping and reshaping of the riverbed as the river wanders its floodplain—all those critical functions, stilled and starved by the dams for so long, will resume.

The dams monkey-wrenched those workings of the river, diverting its energy to turn turbines, making electric power for us. Unplugging the dams would once again let the river do its own work instead of ours, and put its energy back into this watershed. The Elwha has so much to catch up on: moving a hundred years' worth of wood and gravel downstream; building and moving channels; conveying and nurturing the fish that feed a vast web of life long starved for nutrients from the sea. From the slime on the river rocks to the bears bustling in the mountain berry bushes, from the trees in the uplands to the bugs feeding the birds singing in them—all were once nourished by the river, and could be again.

As fish populations rebuild, salmon will feed the watershed. The soils, the trees, the bears, the bobcats, the birds, even the tiny invertebrates in the gravel will feast. Today, only in the lower Elwha River below the dams, a few weeks of the year when the big fish are coming back, is some hint of the river's original raucous productivity on display, with eagles and ospreys in the trees, seals cruising the river mouth, and gulls, mergansers, and river otters moving in for a meal. It's that whole catenation of thrashing, singing, swimming, noisy, feasting, rotting life that it is hoped dam removal will bring back.

Especially above the dams in the national park, nature still has plenty to work with. Even today, the quiet pools in these braided side channels are alive with resident trout. As McMillan silked his fly atop a shaded pool, a popping sound broke the morning quiet. Blammo, one fish hit after another, and in fifteen minutes McMillan caught at least half a dozen small rainbow trout. He hefted the fish in a five-gallon plastic bucket full of river water across the sandbar to Morley, who dumped a slug of clove oil in the water. In moments, the fish rolled over, alive and well but anesthetized enough to be handled.

Kneeling in the sand, working quickly, Morley reached in the bucket and pulled out a trout. Rainbows live up to their name: silvery, with a pronounced lateral line and tiny spots, they were gleaming and bright, the river's jewelry, scattering sunlight. "So pretty," Morley said. "I love these fish." But Morley, a research fishery biologist with NOAA's Northwest Fisheries Science Center in Seattle, has seen plenty of trout, and she got right down to business. She measured the trout, then poked a large plastic syringe into its mouth, pumping its stomach gently with a stream of water. "We want to know what prey is available for the fish, and we think that will change a lot," Morley said. As she spoke, Exhibit A upchucked its breakfast: a wad of bugs gleaned from the river that morning. "I've got the mother lode here," Morley said, picking apart a gooey mass in her palm. "Ant, crane-fly larvae, adult mayfly, winged adult caddis fly."

Morley had been working on the Elwha since 2004, studying its "inverts"—the underwater realm of invertebrate life. Hers is a world of minute things that do big things, such as periphyton. Easy to dismiss as mere slime, it's the grassland of the river, a vast pasture of algae, fungi, and bacteria on the river's bottom. Stoked by sunlight, it is a year-round standing crop of nutrients at the base of the food chain that feeds everything else. "It starts with the slime, and that feeds the grazers:

algae feeders, like little cows of the stream bottom," Morley said. Here, she explained, is where all the primary production happens: Shredders, such as stone flies, break down the leaves falling in the river into tiny particulate organic matter. Filterers, such as caddis flies, thrive on that fine material, building minute houses on the river bottom, where they weave delicate nets to filter their meal from the current. They emit a high-pitched screech to scare off competitors. That's just for starters. A fearsome nation, the river's invertebrates are endowed with features straight out of science fiction. The water teems with nymphs with extendable jaws to reach out and grab prey and propulsion mechanisms to zip them around, pushing water out their rumps. Each animal has its niche, grazing, shredding, and filtering, in a little-noticed underwater wonderland of creatures and interrelationships that link the aquatic and terrestrial worlds.

To learn what food is available for fish before dam removal, Morley was relying on two methods: staking a seine across a stretch of river to capture invertebrates drifting in the current, and gently pumping the stomachs of the fish the team caught to see what the fish were eating. She was as interested in what was falling in the water from the overhanging trees as what was produced in the river, to inform her question of how food sources for fish would change over time. As she pulled her gear, she rinsed the net through a sieve, putting the material caught in it into bottles filled with ethanol to analyze back at the lab. "We think the prey that is available for fish will change a lot," she said. "There will be lots of sediment [released in the short term], so they may rely more on terrestrial [food] sources [during this period of high turbidity]. Once you know about it, you see how everything is intimately connected."

Ahead of them in the channel, dressed like Ninja Turtles in their dry suits, Keith Denton, also with NOAA, and Daniel Hernandez, a NOAA intern, got into the water for a snorkel survey of anything swimming. Dreamy work where the channel flows deep, it quickly turned to a belly crawl, with Denton rolling on his side and taking his mouthpiece out to call out every fish he found to Hernandez, logging the tally from the banks. For the snorkeler in the team—they took turns—it was an inch-by-inch task, poking headfirst under root wads and probing back eddies barely deep enough to float in.

While they worked I walked alone up the banks of a side channel of the Elwha, following it to its source. Here was a pellucid stream fed by a groundwater spring, flowing year-round into the side channel. In the silent realm below the silvery surface of these quiet waters, caddis flies trundled across the sandy bottom, their bodies in cases to protect their tasty larval form. The roots of trees, a shocking magenta—who ever would have expected that?—reached into the water, waving like wind socks in the current. Shadows moved over the sandy bottom as water striders scooted over the surface. Their gossamer legs danced on the stage of the water's surface tension, a light and airy backwoods ballet in miniature.

Water tumbled over a branch, driving silver bubbles of fresh oxygen into a plunge pool of cold, clean water. This was not the Elwha of the whitewater kayaking films, blasting furious through rock canyons. Here, drama played out on a small scale, as tiny sticks and bark caught in jams of branches that made eddies in the flow. A juvenile fish no longer than the joint of my finger wiggled into the pool beneath the branch, facing upstream as a cluster of alder cones swished by overhead on the water's surface. Threads of algae streamed like hair in the

Sarah Morley of NOAA's Northwest Fisheries Science Center in Seattle places a net in a side channel of the Elwha to sample invertebrates in the water. Her research is focused on the river's food web.

With barely enough water to float in, a researcher zipped into a dry suit snorkels a side channel of the Elwha to help assess the baseline fish population in the river prior to dam removal.

current as the water eased downstream, alive with drifting seeds, detritus, and bugs. Leaf litter cartwheeled down the fine, sandy streambed. The shredded bits tumbled down a mosaic of pebbles on the bottom, overlain with the rippling reflections of sunlight. I realized as I watched that the woven pattern of the current, visible in the surface of the water, was mirrored in the stem and vein pattern of the alder leaves, the stem and branch pattern of the sword ferns, and the tiny branched shapes of the moss on the banks. Land and water interwove and interacted at every scale and dimension of the Elwha.

. . .

The sun was dipping lower. It was time to head back to camp. On the way I crossed paths with Hernandez, who had unpeeled from his dry suit and was walking down to the river to fill the spaghetti pot from the Elwha. He and Morley started getting dinner together as Pess headed to the main stem of the river, fly rod in hand. The sun, dipping into the tree line, threw a last scatter of light over the river, its thick gold gleam shot through with the glistening webs of ballooning spiders. The Elwha's crossing currents wove a complex pattern, tight as a basket. "Whoa, that was a big fish!" Pess yelled as something hefty tested his line. He cast and cast again, his line singing, as a fat full moon rose above the trees. But up here, above the dams, the most he would catch were resident trout. Even below the dams, where the salmon and steelhead still come back, salmon populations in 2011 were estimated to be at about 1 percent of their pre-dam numbers. Pinks were down to returns of fewer than one hundred fish, chum fewer than two hundred. Sockeye are extinct (though kokanee, their freshwater life-form, exist in healthy populations in Lake Sutherland and are

expected to help kick-start a sockeye run, once the dams are out). Eulachon are listed for protection in the Elwha under the federal Endangered Species Act, as are steelhead, Puget Sound chinook, and bull trout. Nearly all of the chinook, coho, and steelhead in the river today are hatchery raised.

Dick Goin of Port Angeles knew a very different river, and not that long ago. He first saw the Elwha when his family moved to Port Angeles in 1937, when he was six years old. Back then, fifty- and sixty-pound salmon were commonly landed in the Elwha, and every fish was over twenty pounds. "When we came here, these salmon sustained us, and they became a big part of my life," said Goin, a retired machinist who at eighty has lived intimately with this river most of his adult life. A gentle, kind-faced man who takes to wearing blue jeans with wide suspenders, it had pained him to witness the river's slow decline. "How do you explain to somebody there are two fish here now, but there used to be four hundred? You can't miss what you never saw, but to me, that just means you need to work harder."

His family didn't know anything about salmon, being from the Midwest. But as a kid he went to the same school as the tribal kids, so he learned about fishing the lower river, where his family had moved. The deer had already been hunted out as the Depression bit down hard, but the salmon were still plentiful. "When the tide came in at the right time of year, you could actually stand there and watch the bottom turn gray with salmon; that is how many there were," Goin said. "This river was really alive then. Sometimes there was enormous amounts of pinks, and you saw just hundreds of gulls. There were otters, and of course it brought the bears. You should have heard it; it was incredibly noisy, all this going on. The

Biologists snorkeling the Elwha know the river's secret worlds of intimate beauty, where the light is soft and the water is clear, clean, and cold.

bears came sometimes in daylight but mostly after dark; it was very common to see them fishing. There were herons and eagles; one time on the clay bank, I saw a carcass on a logjam, and there was even a cougar that came along and got it. He didn't mind getting his feet wet for a meal like that. We had surf smelt and eulachon that went as far up the river as a mile and a half. And lampreys. When we were fishing late steelhead in the river—it was always open—we would hook them [lamprey]. They didn't bite, but then you had this creature you didn't really want but you didn't want to handle either. There were sturgeon too.

"It's a quiet river now; we no longer see the hundreds of salmon throwing themselves at the dam. No fish jumping, no hordes of birds, no bears. No battle among the giant male kings, no huge redds [spawning nests] dug by the Elwha females, no quiet pools full of Elwha salmon, no hordes of insects." He remembers catching eighteen wild steelhead in an hour in one riffle and runs of pinks in the 1930s and 1940s and even into the 1950s that were spectacular, as much as a quarter million fish.

It is hard to even imagine the abundance of the river before the dams. But the historical record offers some clues. Early explorers, jaded by the droves of black-tailed deer, elk, bears, and wolves they encountered in the Olympics, exclaimed in their journals over the massive runs of fish and the ruckus they raised. Some complained they could hardly sleep in the

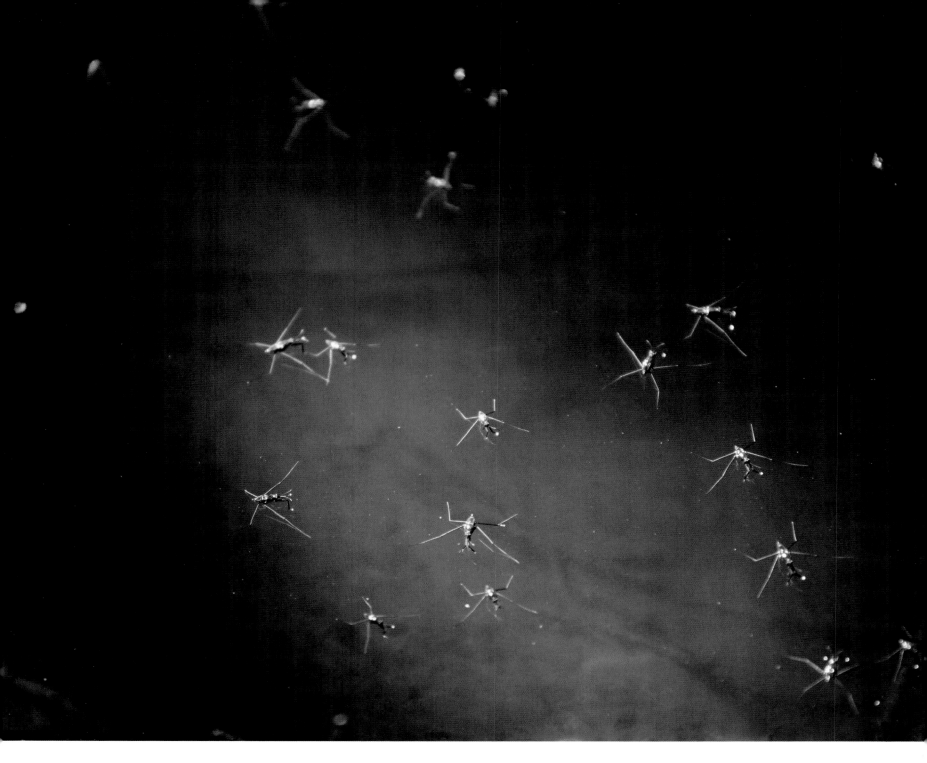

Riding the surface tension of a backcountry tributary stream of the Elwha, these water striders are a tiny, delicate part of the wheels within wheels of the river's complex ecology.

George Pess, left, of NOAA's Northwest Fisheries Science Center in Seattle, leads an interagency team studying the river before and after dam removal. A campfire lights his work, planning the next day's survey of the river in the summer of 2010.

summer and fall if they unfurled bedrolls riverside during the salmon runs.

Private Harry Fisher, a member of an expedition mounted by the US Army and the Oregon Alpine Club, wrote of making camp along the Queets River, the Elwha's muscular cousin to the southwest, the afternoon of September 25, 1890. In his unpublished handwritten manuscript, "Lt. O'Neil's Exploration of the Olympic Mountains" (on microfilm in its entirety at the University of Washington Libraries Special Collections, including his whimsical hand-drawn sketches), Fisher describes his night by the river:

I found a beautiful camping ground directly above the reception of a small tributary from the west. . . . I had not long to wait until I had a chinook salmon weighing about forty pounds. Several water ouzels perched on the rocks near me as if realizing that I would leave them the lion's share. That was the first occasion in which I heard water ouzel sing. One warbled beautifully and in clear notes seemingly happy at the bounteous feast before them. Cutting off enough for supper and breakfast, I had scarcely moved ten feet away before three of them were pecking at the flesh remaining. This camp I registered Camp Skookum. Although warm and comfortable I might as well have selected a camp in Barnum's menagerie so far as sleep was concerned. Located near a shoal in the stream great salmon threshed in the water all night long in their efforts to ascend the stream. Wild animals which I could not see snapped the bushes in all directions traveling up and down in search of fish. At every few yards was to be seen the remains of a fish where cougar, coon, otter, or eagle had made meal.

But as we made our camp on that perfect August moonlit night by the Elwha, the only salmon in the river's middle and upper watershed were in Indian elders' stories and explorers' journals. It was getting dark, and I started gathering firewood from the beach and gravel bar in front of our campsite. Gnarled, twisted river teeth and bits of blasted root wads long since detonated by the river from its banks were sun-baked to perfection for our campfire. Night fell, and the first stars pricked out of the velvet black dark. But it was too quiet. As we unrolled sleeping bags to camp in the wilderness of the Elwha River's upper reaches, no slapping tails roiled the water during what should have been the height of the summer salmon run. And in the morning, there were no eagles in the trees, no footprints of bears, no river otter tracks on the sandy banks—and no salmon in the river above the dams.

A keystone species, wild salmon—the animal that in every life stage helps feed this wilderness, from birds to bugs to salamanders to bears to cougars (yes, Barnum's menagerie)—had been gone for a century.

The Elwha runs wild and free within Olympic National Park, above the former site of Glines Canyon Dam.

2
ELWHA

The Elwha is many rivers. It has a distinct conformation, flowing through a landscape that alternates between tight, solid rock canyons and broad, flat valleys. It flows not just in the main channel but also in many rippling, green glides and side channels of the river, twining around logjams and joined by quiet, spring-fed tributary streams so clear the water is like a lens into the aqueous wonderland under the surface. Dancing with light, the river's shove to salt water has an inexorable and inexhaustible energy, an insistence only the push of the wind matches. Glacier-fed, cold, clean, in its main channel it runs steep and deep, glowing with glacial sediments that tint the water aquamarine in the sun, teal in the shadows.

The Elwha flows north, to the saltwater Strait of Juan de Fuca. Lake Sutherland, to the left, used to be home to a native sockeye run now extinct. With the dams out, it is hoped sockeye will recolonize the lake.

Born in the southern Bailey Range of the Olympic Mountains, the Elwha is the crown jewel of a wild ecosystem. With eight major tributaries, more than 115 miles of its silvery fingers reach into a 321-square-mile watershed. It is a uniquely remote place. Few other national parks in the country boast Olympic National Park's isolation. No road cuts across the Olympic range, and the region's mostly drippy, dreary, foggy climate makes it too cloudy for helicopter tourism. Listening is one of the great pleasures of this place: to the buzzing, one-note call of the varied thrush cutting through the fog; to the squeak of Olympic marmots in the high country; to the crash of elk running through the forested valley bottoms. And, always, there is the river. Sometimes distant, sometimes near and loud enough to make it hard to talk, it's the constant companion and signature sound of this wilderness valley.

One of the park's ten major rivers, all as beautiful as their names, the Elwha spirals down from the Olympics along with the Dosewallips, the Duckabush, Skokomish, and Quinault. The Queets. Hoh. Bogachiel, Dungeness, and Sol Duc. Rising no higher than about 8000 feet above sea level from the surrounding lowlands, the Olympics nonetheless cast a rain shadow that bequeaths to the Elwha some of its special qualities. Because the Elwha runs in the lee of the high Olympics, it is less vulnerable to the floods that scour its western counterparts, such as the Hoh and the Queets. Yet the upper reaches of the Elwha watershed still stack plenty of snow. Good, cold, year-round flows nourish aquatic life that, combined with the large amounts of fish that used to storm the Elwha, can sustain a river system of unusual fecundity and productivity.

The precipitation the Elwha watershed receives varies drastically, from about 220 inches a year, mostly falling as snow in

Using backpack electroshockers, biologists briefly stun fish in the river so they can be collected and sampled. In this side channel below Elwha Dam scientists found juvenile rainbow trout, coho salmon, and sculpin.

In addition to its muscular main channel, the Elwha branches into more than 26 miles of quiet side channels that provide important nursery and spawning habitat for fish. These scientists are working in a side channel shaded by a graceful alder colonnade.

the upper basin, to about 56 at the river mouth. Vegetation steps in terraces up from the river, with willow and alders dominating the disturbed zones closest to it, and Douglas fir, western hemlock, and western red cedar gracing the lower-elevation forests above. There are grand old-growth trees here, particularly in the Godkin and Slate Creek valleys, with tops of Douglas firs too far out of sight to see from the forest floor, and great candelabra-shaped cedars. Wildlife ranges from the tiniest winter wrens, belting out their complex arpeggios from deep in the forest, to the haunting, rhythmic beat of drumming grouse.

As we studied maps and talked with the team of scientists working on the river, it became clear the Elwha had to be understood as three distinct realms: the upper river, the middle river, and the lower river. Above the 210-foot-high Glines Canyon Dam, the gateway to the unspoiled upper Elwha, and on up to the headwaters at about 4500 feet elevation is the wildest stretch of the river. Up here, beyond the influence of either of the dams, the river still muscles through the landscape, carving through rock canyons, calving off chunks of sandstone cliffs, tumbling giant trees into the flow as it jumps channels, avulsing and chewing off its own banks. The middle river is squeezed between the slightly less than 9 miles between the two dams. The lower river, below the 108-foot-tall Elwha Dam, is the Elwha's remaining 5-mile run to salt water—and for a century, until the dams started to come down, was the only portion of the river available to salmon. The Elwha Dam cut the fish off from 90 percent of their habitat with the beginning of construction in 1910.

These three segments of the river turned out to be very different. It's one thing to study the varied realms of the Elwha on a map and another to experience them. I was surprised, as we explored the river over two field seasons with the scientists, by the river's wondrous complexity and diversity. In time, we would hike its luxuriant upland forests, explore the wind-blasted beach where the Elwha meets the Strait of Juan de Fuca, and traverse much of the main stem of the river in

"You are only as good as your data" was the motto of the interagency team of scientists led by George Pess of NOAA Fisheries seeking to document the baseline condition of the Elwha and its response after dam removal.

Field research in the Elwha is no easy task. Nets break, the current kicks like an irritable mule, and the river is too wild to work in much of the year. NOAA intern Daniel Hernandez struggles to set a seine in the current.

Snorkeling becomes a belly crawl as a researcher follows a tributary stream to its source in the Elwha's backcountry in the Geyser Valley. The Elwha is refreshed with cold, pure water from countless unnamed backcountry streams and springs.

between. But most of the scientists' work we witnessed was done not in the Elwha's mighty main channel but in places unnamed and unknown to most visitors: the side channels of the Elwha. Secluded, quiet, sheltered, they are the river's spa, where fish go to rest, hide, and feed. Each side channel is different, and no one has closely surveyed them all.

We got to know the river in a series of trips with research scientists, starting with George Pess's interagency team in July 2010. They were sampling pieces of the 10 miles of side channels in the upper river, nearly 8 miles in the middle river

between the two dams, and 5 miles in the lower river. And there were surely even more miles, Pess felt, of the river's total floodplain channel habitat, a fine tracery of branchlets that are the river's nurseries, feeding grounds, and resting places.

The importance of side channel habitat, noted Mike McHenry, habitat biologist for the Lower Elwha Klallam Tribe, had been underestimated even by the biologists. These habitats were not counted when the estimates of potential productivity for the restored Elwha were calculated at about 390,000 returning adult fish. But their importance was becoming clearer as

Bracken fern lifts its lovely head, unfurling tight spring buds. Native plants provide a lush understory to the deep forests that cloak the river's pristine wilderness reaches within Olympic National Park, which protects 83 percent of the Elwha watershed.

research progressed. McHenry was one of the biologists who had logged the most hours on these monitoring trips, building season by season a more detailed picture of the river, going back at least ten years.

The Northwest's trademark summer morning fog was blowing in from the Strait of Juan de Fuca as we headed out from a trail to the banks of the lower river, on the Lower Elwha Klallam Tribe's reservation. Following the team through Indian plum and salmonberry thickets, we finally broke out of a dense stand of alders into another world: the rocky beach of a side channel of the lower river. I tipped my head back to watch the mist cruise through the canopy of alders laced overhead. The sun was just starting to burn through, reflected from the river's surface in ripples of aqueous light undulating on the colonnade of alders lining the banks. The Elwha slid smooth and green downstream.

"I'd do anything for George," McHenry noted, and I was sure he meant it. As respected for the quality of his science as he is liked for the good chemistry he brings to fieldwork, Pess believes deeply in the role of the public scientist in guiding and informing the recovery work on the Elwha. "Make sure one foot is always stable," Pess called out to me as he stepped into the river to cross to a deep pool. For starters, the goal was to stake out a research unit in this side channel, to count and identify the fish in it by species and size. To do it, the scientists geared up with a backpack electroshocker and a seine to work a segment of the river about 26 feet wide by 115 feet long, to see which method worked better for sampling fish populations. The lower river is the only refuge left in the Elwha for oceangoing fish, and the scientists knew they would find fish here they would see nowhere else in the river, including steelhead and salmon. It was also the stretch of river where scientists expect they will see some of the largest changes over time, as sediment from the upper watershed settles out of the water column where the river's gradient flattens at the end of its run.

"It's like a party back here," said Keith Denton as he poked a net under a root wad where the fish were thick in the 47-degree-Fahrenheit water. "Under the logjams, it looks like an aquarium," he added as Jeff Duda, a research ecologist for the US

The Elwha runs 45 miles from its headwaters in the Olympic Mountains in Washington State to the Strait of Juan de Fuca. Before construction of the dams the river was alive with ten different runs of salmon and steelhead.

Geological Survey (USGS) Western Fisheries Research Center in Seattle worked the electroshocker. "All right. Shocking," Duda said, as he gave the river another jolt. "There's definitely some along the back there," Denton said, closing in with the net, working every pool and rivulet. Sculpins. Coho. Rainbow trout. Pess came over with a five-gallon plastic bucket and collected the fish. He stuck a fish-tank aerator in it, run off a battery, and a shake of clove oil to mildly stun the fish so they could be handled and measured. They would let the fish recover in the bucket for a while before returning them to the river—after clipping a fin so they'd know if they recaptured the same fish.

As we got to know the lower river, below the first dam, the word *habitat* seemed so inadequate for the complexity of this place. Even within just one side channel, there is a universe of variables: Gradient. Pool depth. Overhead vegetation. Sunlight exposure. Temperature. Turbidity. Wood deposition. Water quality. The very function and composition of the food chain. Then there are all the variables in the wider systems of which the river is a part: the marine environment, the changing climate, and all the other elements we humans throw into the mix, from hatchery fish that will still be stocked in the Elwha to man-made alteration of the floodplain, including levees that imprison the river as it nears the sea. The levees were actually made even longer and higher in the restoration project, to protect adjacent property owners from flooding. But above the levees, once the dams were out, the river would finally be allowed to be messy, ever-changing, tangled, complex, in an interwoven system of feedback loops within more loops, from the hydrologic cycle to the twenty-four-hour clock, the seasonal gyre, and evolving genetics and behavior of every living being in the system. None of it is isolated from the other parts, or static—like, say, a levee or a dam.

I was struck too, watching Pess and the team work, by how hard it is to ever actually know anything about any of it. Not to generate a computer model, but to stand there in 50-degree water all day, holding a measuring stick; to physically map the depths of all the pools in the floodplain channels and sample the size of the rocks on the bottom; to set a documented baseline in order to know how the river would change over time. And even this team, with more than ten years of effort and more than a dozen people hard at it, would never see and measure and understand it all. The most even they could hope for was a snapshot, a sense of what this river, on the verge of such a profound change, was like.

■ ■ ■

Beginning in July 2011 we joined the team in several field trips to the middle river, breaststroking through chest-high sword ferns, way off trail, to reach a side channel between the dams. As I walked, I trailed the backs of my hands over the cool, wet ferns, soothing nettle stings from the morning's hike in from the trailhead.

Unlike the first floodplain channel in the lower river, this one was fed entirely by groundwater. And what a difference that made. With no gradient to induce flow, at this time of year in midsummer the water was perfectly still and clear. It was an important place to explore. During the first years of dam removal, the clear, clean water in groundwater channels like these was expected to be critical to fish seeking escape from the sediment-choked main stem. Groundwater-fed side channels also have always been important temperature moderators.

The spectacular color of the Elwha is a product of glacial meltwater. The river peaks in its flow during the spring melt off and winter storms. Chinook salmon, the largest in the river, evolved to master the powerful main channel.

They can be 10 degrees warmer than the glacial meltwater-fed main stem in winter, giving young fish a tranquil, warm, sheltered environment where they can grow bigger faster, boosting their chances for survival. In the summer, the cold groundwater inflow also keeps these floodplain channels at 50 degrees Fahrenheit, just perfect for salmon. Trickles of cold, clear water from the hill slope also fed the channel, joining the groundwater to provide plenty of flow for fish year-round, even after the snowpack had run off.

A mass of salamander eggs showed how amphibians use these still, side channel waters. Here, beneath the mirrored surface, tiny creatures were busily devouring the nutritious litter that rained into the river from the trees above, and periphyton was growing thick as fur on rocks on the bottom of

44 Elwha Dam was one in a series of dams built in Washington during the dam building era of the 1900s through the 1970s, with many rivers including the Columbia, Skokomish, Skagit, White Salmon, and Lower Snake harnessed for hydropower.

the channel. A soft rain began to fall, glazing the sword ferns with more moisture. Wet, mushroom-eared logs were rotted soft as corduroy. I closed my eyes and listened to the rain. Such a sound; it filled my mind. It was a recital of music from the beginning of time, with its own applause as the rain intensified, pattering the leaves. No rain touched me where I sat deep under the forest canopy, yet I heard it everywhere. Fat falling drops made rings in the side channel's glassy surface. Here on display was the water cycle that makes the whole system work: the freshwater easing inexorably down and down, from cloud to rain and snow, from glacier to snowmelt, from rain to spring, seep, groundwater, and stream; sopping the forests, gathering and hastening to the river, carrying along wood and gravel in its flow from the snowfields of the Olympics to the blue salt water of the Strait. The ascending glissando of a Swainson's thrush embellished the meditative quiet of the forest. If there are fairies in the Elwha valley, I felt pretty sure this is where they live.

We walked on to another side channel in which the water was aquamarine and I could no longer see my feet for all the glacial flour in the water. That told me this side channel was influenced not only by groundwater but also, at high flows, by water from the main stem. As I sloshed along, I encountered a fledgling dipper snoozing on the end of a log, utterly unconcerned as I passed. The river's only aquatic songbird, dippers—water ouzels—are named for their habit of dipping up and down as they stand by the riverside between underwater flights to forage for food. The banks were twined with wild roses, their pink petals floating on the water, and tiny, delectable wild strawberries, the fruit no bigger than a fingernail. I remembered stories from elders of the Lower Elwha

Klallam Tribe about gathering strawberries by the river as girls and eating them in saucers of milk. This must have been what they meant. Wands of blooming foxglove waved on the breeze; tangles of salmonberry were spangled with fat, juicy fruit that glowed yellow, orange, and red in the gloaming. I ate berry after berry, watching a swallowtail butterfly on a log open and close its glamorous wings, warming itself in a patch of sun. The fragrances were intoxicating. Wet soil. Berries. Roses.

For all our fascination with the Elwha's side channels, though, we also wanted a chance to feel the rush of boating the main channel. I'd hiked along the Elwha, camped along it, and of course driven by the river every time I traveled up into the park. Steve Ringman had also flown over the Elwha to shoot scenic views for the newspaper. But neither of us until then had been on the Elwha or in it. Pess and McHenry would be floating a reach of the river that runs free between the two dams with a team of scientists in the late spring of 2011. We jumped at the chance to come along.

The scientists would be setting up monitoring stations along the Elwha to track sediment levels in the river once the dams came down. That meant a raft trip. As Steve and I drove into the outfitter's lot, tires spitting gravel, our guide, a rugged-looking young lady in a chain-saw bill cap, nailed us before we even got out of our cars as the city slickers from Seattle. She matter-of-factly divided all of us into teams, wisely hopping into our raft to row instead of handing the oars to either Steve or me. Two teams of scientists took the other rafts: geomorphologists, geologists, and biologists from NOAA's Northwest Fisheries Science Center in Seattle, the Lower Elwha Klallam Tribe, and the US Bureau of Reclamation from California and Colorado settled into our bobbing yellow rubber rafts and left terra firma.

It was the wind that hit us first.

Out here, in the exposed main channel of the river, the Elwha seemed to make its own wind, blowing up the valley as we swung out into the fullness of the river's flow. Good-bye, quiet side channels and crystal-clear springs: this was going to be a very different experience—especially this year. It was late spring, and the snow was thick on the Olympics, loaded with 200 percent of average snowpack from the winter of 2010–11. A howler, it had been followed by a stubborn cold spring. I already regretted choosing a wet suit over waterproof waders. The wind pushed into the neoprene, wet within minutes as the glacial meltwater of the Elwha slopped over the side of the raft.

The current rocked and swept us along, grinding us into the bank, tree roots poking out at eye level. I saw one of the scientists go over the side of her raft to lighten the load and get the raft off the rocks where it had stranded. A stiff sacrifice even in waders in 45-degree water; she was dripping as they pulled her back onboard.

With field time so precious, they drove themselves hard, making the most of every minute of daylight. They were in and out of the rafts, up and down the riverbanks, sledgehammering in rebar to mark future monitoring sites. Years later, someone will read data, neatly arrayed in crisp, white scientific papers still warm off the printer or glowing bright and tidy on their screen, with no idea what it took these scientists, shrink-wrapped in waders and neoprene, to get it.

Pacific tree frogs called from the forest, and big-leaf maples dangled white garlands of bloom revving up to become helicopter-bladed seeds. The alders were lime green with new leaves. I heard something—traffic? No, of course not. Not here. That roar, louder as we slid nearer, was . . . rapids. "This might be a little rocky," our guide said cheerfully. What was all that she had told us before we got in the rafts? Something about stay with the boat if you flip? Or was it . . . get away from the boat if you flip?

We twirled, bobbed, and slingshotted backward down the river, swirling in teal and aquamarine water frothing with white standing waves. The soft green, mossy banks of the river swished past. Sun steamed mist from the grass. The cold water was so clear, we could watch the rocks parade under our rafts as we sped over their colors and forms. My feet, in neoprene booties, were aching in the cold water splashing over us as the raft caromed from rock to rock. I gripped the bucking raft with one hand and held my notepad high over my head with the other, like a bull rider shot out of a rodeo chute. "Whew!" our guide said as the rapids released us. "That's the first time I've done that without following someone. That was some rock garden! How about when we spun the boat?" She muscled into the oars as a harlequin duck watched, unperturbed. Behind it on the bank lay an alder felled by a beaver, the stump newly gnawed through, wood chips piled thickly around the trunk.

With a bump, we pulled up to the bank and the scientists headed off to slam more rebar in the ground, marking another monitoring site. I curled in a sunny spot on river rocks for heat, then—feeling bruised and river-bashed—moved to a stump, its mossy top deep and plush as a down pillow in a velvet case. Sword ferns all around me were big enough to lie down across, inviting a nap. Somewhere back in the woods, I heard the sledgehammering stop: time to get back in the rafts.

We heaved ourselves off the rocks to ride the current until we eased around a bend into a deep, still, green pool. "The swimming hole," said our guide, telling us it was just 7 feet

The Elwha estuary and near shore are limited in ecological function and starved for sediment by levees and dams. Those problems were only partially addressed and in some ways worsened by the Elwha restoration, which extended and raised levees for flood protection.

As Lake Aldwell drained, an otherworldly, liminal landscape emerged that was no longer lake, but not the forest it once was, or might one day become. The author marvels at a massive stump still marked by the scars from loggers' springboards.

deep here; floating on top of the seemingly bottomless glowing green water, it felt like 100. Moss on the banks grew all the way to the waterline, green meeting more green, all of it overhung by gardens of ferns on wet black rocks. The fragrance of cottonwood found us. Shreds of moss trailed from the sleeve of the sweater I had pulled on over my soggy wet suit. Twigs had pushed into its weave; bits of leaf crunched in my hair. Alder cones dangling from a sweeper tickled at my ear as we cut close to shore. Suddenly, as we rowed along, the river started to die.

Silt and sediment snuffed the stately procession of colored rocks sliding by under our boat, an undifferentiated sludgy bottom taking its place. As it shallowed, the river's teal green color was lost along with its depth. The river's dancing light switched off, too, along with its current as we drifted into a still, brown pond. This was yet another distinct habitat of the Elwha, that was for sure. But this one was not natural. We had arrived at Lake Aldwell, above the Elwha Dam.

Elwha Dam was built by Thomas Aldwell not to serve existing demand, but to attract industrial development to the Olympic Peninsula with the lure of cheap hydropower. His was the entrepreneurial spark that electrified the Port Angeles economy.

3

THE NIAGARA OF THE PACIFIC

In Thomas Aldwell's day, newspapers were the main way people kept in touch. There were small, feisty newspapers everywhere. And Aldwell, the man who built the Elwha Dam, clipped them obsessively. To read his personal scrapbooks, preserved at the University of Washington Libraries Special Collections, is to know something of the man. Turn the thick, black construction-paper pages, see his blue pencil marking the paragraphs of the pasted-up articles he liked best—and notice, too, what he left out.

Thomas Aldwell hams it up in a studio shot published in his autobiography, *Conquering the Last Frontier*. His original caption: "Tom Aldwell in the early days when he drove claim jumpers off his homestead on the Elwha River." (Courtesy, Noreen Frink)

Aldwell arrived in Port Angeles in 1890 with $500 in his pocket. A swashbuckling pioneer with relentless ambition, he soon decided to take this ragged little stump-pocked frontier town with cattle roaming the streets and upbuild it to a boomtown that would live up to its name, the Gateway City. Upbuild. It was a term I had never heard until reading the newspapers Aldwell had clipped, and it was in story after story about the industrial development of the raw land of the Olympic Peninsula. To upbuild was to dredge, dike, fill, drain, farm, plow, dam, mine, and log. To upbuild was to convert the natural abundance of the region to the cash rewards of a resource-extraction-based economy.

As closely in his personal scrapbooks as Aldwell had documented the transformation of the region and his own role in it, his omissions can be no oversight. He had built his dam illegally, on a wink and a nod carefully worked out over many months of correspondence with state fisheries officials, but you won't find that in his scrapbooks or in his personal papers either, also on file at the Special Collections. No, for Aldwell's special deal, you have to look in the Washington State Archives in Olympia, amid the death rattle of onionskin typing paper. Aldwell's fountain-pen signature on his correspondence with a series of state fisheries officials, with his trademark flourish of three dots underneath his name penned for extra flair, fits the man who brushed off the state requirement that any dam must provide a fish way "wherever fish are wont to ascend." It was a law that had been on the books since Washington was a territory.

First documented by Bruce Brown in his landmark book *Mountain in the Clouds*, the sorry tale of the state's sellout of the Elwha for Aldwell's dam is well known by now. Aldwell didn't even need to come up with the arrangement that allowed him to skirt the law. State fish commissioner Leslie Darwin did it for him, offering in a letter of August 17, 1913, to let Aldwell's dam do double duty as an obstruction the state could use to take fish at the foot of the dam for a hatchery. All Aldwell had to do was donate the land and build the hatchery, never mind bothering with the trouble and expense of constructing a fish ladder over the 108-foot-high dam. "My plan forever eliminates bother in the future," Darwin wrote Aldwell on August 21, 1913, offering to substitute a hatchery for habitat. For the state of Washington, it was to become a hundred-year habit from which wild salmon have yet to recover.

The hatchery soon failed, and the state gave up on the fish and walked away from the river. Aldwell, interestingly, never quite got around to turning over the deed for the land. That's not in the scrapbooks either. But what is, in page after page, is the excitement that crackled in town about the dam and the promise of industrial development the peninsula had so longed for. The newspapers swooned over "Tommy," the daredevil entrepreneur betting his all on Port Angeles. As for the Elwha—dubbed "the Niagara of the Pacific"—it was merely waiting, in the thinking of the day, to finally be put to productive use. Early engineers, industrialists, and newspaper writers struggled to find words that could adequately capture their enthusiasm for the Elwha's potential for development. Here is William Ware, a Port Angeles engineer who would later sell his homestead claim for development of Glines Canyon Dam, quoted in the *Seattle Post-Intelligencer* on December 1, 1901, in a story headlined "Scenic Wonders of the Picturesque Elwha River":

The grandest river of its size in Washington, beautiful, clear as crystal, rushing down from the snowcapped peaks of the majestic Olympics, through gorges, over cataracts, through and among immense boulders, cool and pure and powerful, containing the energy of thousands upon thousands of horsepower, it carries along upon its crest the mighty monarch of the forest as easily as it does the tiny Indian canoe. The Elwha, sublime in its majestic and awe-inspiring scenery, is destined to become a mighty power for good in the hands of ingenious humanity, for the present and future generations.... There is no river in Washington with the *grand future before it, with its immense possibilities, with the undeveloped energy or with the natural facilities that this river has. There are many places along its course where its energy could be transformed into power for the use of the manufacturer, for lighting, for the tramcar, for the streetcar.*

For Aldwell, the dream of the dam started while he was at his desk in the offices of the *Port Angeles Tribune-Times*, where he was managing editor, and he looked up to find a stranger in search of information. Aldwell was used to visitors stopping by as they rolled into town. Port Angeles in 1894 was a wide-open frontier settlement, attracting prospectors, deal makers, and fortune seekers just like him. As the visitor, a developer of one of the first pulp mills on the Youngs River in Oregon—operated by hydropower—told his story, Aldwell suddenly got an idea. "A pulp mill!" Aldwell wrote in his autobiography, the aptly titled *Conquering the Last Frontier*. "I started thinking of mills and what they might mean to Port Angeles. A newspaper could do much to build a town, but industry was what was really needed, and back of industry was power."

In their chance encounter, the river's destiny was set. Aldwell had already staked a claim on the Elwha. His 160 acres included a tight rock canyon, through which the river crashed with all of its power. "I was thinking of the canyon on my claim, recognizing that there was a real power possibility because of the volume of the river and the steep walls of the canyon," Aldwell wrote. "Suddenly the Elwha was no longer a wild stream crashing down to the Strait; the Elwha was peace and power and civilization."

Aldwell by now had chucked his newspaper gig and was crisscrossing the peninsula, signing up power purchasers at a

Thomas Aldwell, third from right, at his Port Angeles real estate office. "I saw Port Angeles was a wild, frontier town," Aldwell wrote in his autobiography. "If I was looking for undeveloped country, I certainly found it." (Courtesy, Noreen Frink)

steel mill near Port Townsend, the Bremerton Navy Yard, and the Army's Fort Worden and Fort Flagler. He went next to the offices of *The Seattle Times*, to meet with publisher Clarence Blethen to drum up support. "[He was] Colonel Blethen to everyone in the Pacific Northwest," Aldwell wrote. "I told him we needed publicity to raise money to build the dam on the Elwha.... I am not sure Blethen was convinced he'd benefit financially by doing this, but he too had an intense feeling for the Pacific Northwest and he agreed to give us publicity.... We

had the active, intelligent support of the press. With the newspaper's support, it wasn't difficult to sell enough additional stock to start financing the dam."

But the real money was back East. On a trip to Chicago, Aldwell next sought the investors he needed to build the dam. He took photographs of the Elwha with him. "I had views of the canyon, the Elwha River, Lake Crescent, and Lake Sutherland. Who could resist them?" Aldwell wrote. "I pointed out the lakes as future reservoirs and the glaciers with summer meltings of the snow that kept the water flowing summer and winter without danger of drying up." As he watched the face of each potential financier, "I could see the magnificence of the country growing on him."

To ragtag Port Angeles, capturing East Coast capital made Aldwell no less than a hero. In Aldwell's scrapbooks is this story, from the *Port Angeles Evening News* January 3, 1939, in a special edition commemorating the twenty-fifth anniversary of the dedication of the power plant, under the headline "Drama and Joy Mark Anniversary. Electric Era marked starting point for real development of Port Angeles and Clallam County":

Tommy Aldwell invaded the offices of the business tycoons of Chicago and other eastern money marts. Those were the days when the big boys sank to their ankles in deep Chinese rugs, dangled monster watch chain charms, and peered at applicants for funds through smoke screens from big black cigars. Into this aura of big money went Tommy. For days the big fellows were not impressed. They couldn't see what good it would do to invest their money in any toy power plant out where the West dipped into the Pacific. They yawned. They puffed. They said "no" so many times that Tommy nearly wore himself out bouncing between the hotel and their offices. Yet in the end he won out and came home with adequate funds to finish the dam.

As construction got underway, the local papers rooted for the project. The idea of a skeptical press misses the tenor of the times and even the purpose of the papers, as embraced by their owners, to—yes—upbuild their respective regions. Consider this gem saved by Aldwell, clipped from the *Port*

Elwha Dam site, 1910. Pictured in the canyon are the original bridge and the start of construction on the power plant. Note the utter lack of safety protection for workers dangling on a platform over the river. (Courtesy, Nippon Paper Industries, Inc.)

Townsend Morning Leader, published as Aldwell readied for construction on August 31, 1910, under the headline "Cause for Congratulation":

"Any man in Port Townsend who knowingly throws as much as a straw in the way of the complete success of the Olympic Power and Development Company should receive the unqualified censure of a united community and should be consigned to the catalogue of undesirables of which this city in company with every community in the state of Washington already has too many. Here's to Tommy Aldwell and to his Olympic Power and Development Company! May they live long and prosper."

Workers wore no protective gear as they labored—no hard hats or even safety lines when working on scaffolding. More than one worker lost his life falling in the cold, swift river. (Courtesy, Nippon Paper Industries, Inc.)

The Seattle Times was just as enthralled, writing as construction progressed on May 1, 1911: "Far down in the canyon cut through the rock by the Elwha in its centuries-long course to the seas appeared the evidence of man's ingenuity in harnessing nature.... Up rearing high in the air, a gigantic derrick with mathematical precision lowered slings of earth to the men at work on the coffer dam more than 100 feet below, while the

roar of the machinery vied with that of the river. The . . . Elwha is now under control."

It is not hard to see what everyone was so excited about. Port Angeles boasted a deepwater port nestled within the sheltering arm of the Ediz Hook, a natural sand spit that was a gift, partly, of the sediments ferried down from the mountains by the Elwha River. But there had been little reason for ships to call in the harbor, with virtually no industry to speak of until the development of hydropower. With post offices in tree stumps and homesteaders hacking a living out of the forest, Port Angeles remained at the turn of the twentieth century a raw outpost. The handwritten diary of one settler preserved at the Clallam County Historical Society, penned in 1901, reveals a virtually medieval existence: "Fixed hay wagon. Hauled hay. Planted potatoes. Filled holes. Dug ditch. Cleared land. Finished logging. Pulled stumps. Hauled four barrels of water. Sawed wood. Piled logs. Built a fire. Hauled potatoes and manure." On it went like that, for decades. The only thing that changed was the homesteader's handwriting, gradually weakening and crabbing as he wore out over the years.

Building the dam was a daredevil exercise in rugged mountain engineering and improvisation. Logging-camp-style cook tents and bunkhouses and even a schoolhouse were thrown up in the woods to serve the needs of hundreds of workers, who got the job done using the tools they had and knew best: spar poles and rigging, picks and shovels. Photographs of construction show the near-madness of the risks, with workers swinging out over the mountain canyon on a simple open platform dangling from a rope, or toiling bareheaded and bare-handed on scaffolding without so much as a safety rope over the boiling rapids of the Elwha. Men were swept away

Overall view of construction of Elwha Dam, approximately 1910. Much of it was built with rudimentary equipment: picks, shovels, hand-drills, sledgehammers, and horse-drawn sleds to move cement. (Courtesy, Nippon Paper Industries, Inc.)

in the powerful current. Cables snapped, killing men where they stood.

A story in a February 17, 1911, newspaper clipping on file at the Clallam County Historical Society—unfortunately, with no name on the newspaper—provides a look at just one casualty: "Man falling in stream has no more chance than he would if falling off top high building" notes the headline. The story recounts:

Mr. [Johanes] Bengston fell into the river from a timber spanning the stream upon which he was working, the fall being but a few foot, but the current is swift and the river treacherous and although he swam downstream for nearly

Construction workers and loggers toiling in the remote country of the Elwha valley lived in rugged camps, enduring isolation and harsh mountain weather. (Courtesy, Nippon Paper Industries, Inc.)

or quite fifty yards in an attempt to make the opposite shore, the current carried him into the swirl where the suction is the greatest and he disappeared under the water.

The body was recovered about a half a mile downstream where it floated on a sandbar, after having been in the water four minutes. The side of the head was badly bruised, and the ear torn, and his breast was lacerated and crushed. The unfortunate man was hewing with an adze the timber on which he was standing, and must in some manner have lost his balance and fallen into the stream . . . he had only gone out to the plant the day before to work, and had been there less than twenty-four hours when the accident occurred. He was a ship's carpenter and sailor by profession and accustomed to dangers.

Buried in Ocean View cemetery in Port Angeles, Bengston was, astonishingly, sixty-seven years old and left a wife and two daughters. He was the second employee to drown in the river in three weeks.

As for Aldwell, he was in a state over the poor quality and slow pace of construction of the dam. In telegrams and letters that flew back and forth between Aldwell, his investors, and the chief engineer, he complained bitterly about the lack of adequate equipment and shoddy materials. Donkeys hauled cars of rock blasted out of the canyon, and horse-drawn sleds, rather than rail, were used to move cement. Some twenty men pounded for a year on the rock walls of the dam with hand drills, as the job suffered with one poorly driven steam drill and no air drill at all. Another twenty men hand split rock and handled it in small pieces, instead of using a rock crusher. "The worst waste was throwing cement into the river in thousands

of barrels in place of putting [in] a caisson. And without testing the bottom of the river," Aldwell wrote.

It was a remark that proved prescient. A few months later, on Halloween night 1912, Aldwell's worst fears were confirmed when the dam, built without pinning its foundation into bedrock, blew out overnight, sending a torrent of water downstream and scouring the riverbed to a depth of 80 feet. Under the headline "Mighty Elwha Breaks Loose From Bondage," the *Olympic Leader* reported on Friday, November 1, 1912:

The outbreak came just before seven o'clock and practically without warning. Within ten minutes after the first sign of danger, the flood was at its worst. With a crash and a roar the wall of steel piling driven just below the dam was carried away and the water spouted up from under the masonry half as high as the dam. So fast did the water come that it filled the canyon below to the height of half a hundred feet and flooded the powerhouse to half its height. Several million feet of logs had been held in booms just above the plant.

When the water began to move, one after another of these booms broke and the logs came surging against the dam. They were caught in the powerful suction and went thru the hole like rabbits under a log. Borne on the torrent as it dashed into the canyon wall and was thrown back against the powerhouse, the logs battered in the west end of the building and pounded to pieces all that beautiful machinery in the generating room. The great dynamos, the switchboards—everything is demolished. The dynamo room is filled with debris—logs, rocks, and mud. The turbines, in another room, were uninjured . . . so fast did the water rise that it was with difficulty the men climbed up the ladder

Built during a grand industrial age in America, the dams were replete with beautiful instrumentation, kept at a high polish and in perfect working order by a crew that took pride in their craft.

fast enough to keep out of its way. The water was nearly 30 feet deep in the turbine room. After the water subsided, a number of big trout were picked up in this room.

The great wall of water, rolling before it a tremendous quantity of debris, went crashing down the valley with the noise of a heavy thunderstorm. Trees along the bank were snapped off and broken up and carried along in the flood. Struck by this avalanche of water and trees, the lower bridge went out with one great crash, checking the motion of the mass not in the slightest. Not a sliver remains that there was ever a bridge at this point. From the wreckage left in the trees along the stream, it is clear that the first rush of water and debris must have been at least 30 feet high. The farmers in the lower valley were warned by phone and fled to the hills for safety. There they built a great fire and stayed about it until ten o'clock, when most of them returned to their homes.... The receding waters left great numbers of salmon and trout strewn over the fields and through the woods, and everyone going down that way got all the fish they could carry home.*

It was a setback, to be sure, but Aldwell was not deterred, putting men to work immediately to plug the hole with great mattresses of fir trees, sunk with 60,000 yards of rock ballast that had been blasted out of the canyon with sixteen tons of dynamite, then covered with soil and gravel. "Monster Blasts Signal Completion of Power Plant" was the headline in the November 5, 1913, *Tribune-Times*. In his autobiography Aldwell wrote of his gratitude for a winter storm as he visited the dam to view its completion; the rain hid the tears of relief on his face.

On February 12, 1914, the town formally dedicated the new dam. It was a day of high celebration, with a half-holiday declared so everyone could participate. The festivities began with a tour of the dam, and the official program began at 2:00 PM at the Opera House, where, according to the *Tribune-Times*, on February 13, 1914, "The Opera House was packed, the house being darkened, decorated with flags, and illuminated with the juice from the plant in whose honor the celebration was planned." Dignitaries came from all over, from the governor of the state of Washington to bankers and industrialists from Seattle, Tacoma, Bremerton, Port Townsend, and

Victoria, British Columbia—and, of course, all of the city's brass. For entertainment, renowned photographer Asahel Curtis showed scenes of Olympic views on his stereoscope. At 6:00 PM, a banquet was laid for four hundred at the Olympic Hotel "at especially arranged banquet tables spread in the big and beautifully lighted lobby.... The orchestra enlivened the assemblage with popular airs, and the scene was indeed one fair to look upon and of which our little city may well be proud. The Toastmaster announced that he had in reserve an array of buttons, especially prepared, operated by Elwha juice, for the occasion, which he intended to push." The mayor of Port Angeles had the honor of pressing the first one. Next, "Mr. Aldwell was given an ovation and in his talk which followed was visibly affected by the demonstration of pride and appreciation in which he was held by the community." Telegrams of congratulation were read, from Milwaukee, Seattle, Montreal, and San Francisco. And for those who hadn't yet celebrated enough, the crowd went back to the Opera House where, as the story describes, partiers "tangoed the light fantastic."

There was something almost biblical in the sense of the town's celebration of Aldwell's triumph of light over darkness, taming wild nature to man's use. In the February 13, 1914, edition of the *Bremerton Searchlight*, this account of the morning's tour of the dam is telling—particularly in contrast to the celebration held in September 2011, to commemorate turning the dam site back to nature:

Solid buttresses and emplacements of concrete masonry provide a home for a hive of industry. The whirl of mechanics and control of water for development stand where five years ago the only visitor was the casual hunter and sportsman or hardy pioneer who was hewing a home out of the forest wilderness abounding. Five years ago these pioneers packed their flour and bacon into the Elwha on their backs over forest trails. Today Governor Lister and accompanying visitors made the trip with the luxury of big taxicabs and other auto service.

Missing, and apparently deliberately avoided by Aldwell when he clipped the ecstatic review of the dedication ceremonies in the *Tribune-Times*, was the cartoon that illustrated that story: a hand-drawn depiction of the dam, with the caption "Well, it is about time." Perhaps, when he put scissors to the morning paper the day after his big party, that caption was a bit too much of a reminder that this wild mountain river had very nearly bested him. Plugged but still never quite right, the Elwha Dam always would leak.

But markets for the dam's power quickly grew. Hydropower sparked the economic boom Port Angeles had been waiting for, never equaled since. With the coming of hydropower, finally, Port Angeles could market all of its natural advantages: vast swaths of timber, abundant water, the Ediz Hook, and a deepwater natural harbor at the west end of the downtown waterfront.

Seattle timber baron Michael Earles was among the first to seize the opportunity just waiting in Port Angeles, building his Puget Sound Mills and Timber Company east of the foot of Ediz Hook. In full operation by 1914, the Big Mill, as it was known, was the largest of its day anywhere. The mill was a world unto itself, with a monthly payroll of $50,000 to $60,000, not counting men felling timber in the woods. It took the skins of 350 steers just to make the 7-foot-wide belt that drove the mill's main shaft. The Port Angeles harbor was busy with as many as six vessels at a time, taking lumber to all points of the globe.

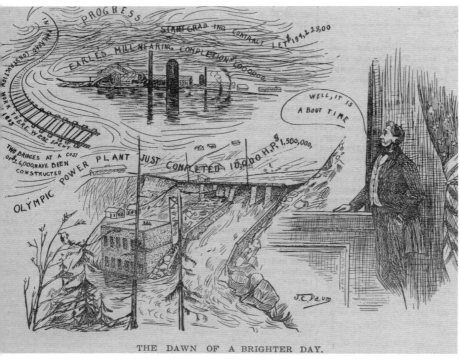

THE DAWN OF A BRIGHTER DAY.

This 1914 newspaper cartoon teases Aldwell, "Well, it is about time." Aldwell was nearly bested by the Elwha, which blew out his 108-foot high dam, requiring reconstruction. (Clallam County Historical Society)

The Seattle Times, on June 19, 1919, raved about the booming city on the peninsula, writing under the headline "Port Angeles Grows as Business Center":

> *Having doffed its swaddling clothes and cast them permanently into the discard, the robust metropolis of the Straits looks confidently forward to the successful consummation of certain projects fraught with cardinal interest not only to herself but the entire northern section of the Olympic Peninsula.... The inception of Port Angeles' commercial growth dates from the construction of the great hydroelectric power plant on the Elwha River... its completion and the awakening of the community from its industrial lethargy were synchronous. The puissant force of the great river running unbridled and unsubdued for countless centuries needed only to be harnessed to start the wheels of industry in motion ... the transition from comparative obscurity to the present healthy condition has been rapid, at times almost sensational.*

But Aldwell was far from finished. He worked next with other boosters to attract the Zellerbach Paper Company from California, which would in 1919 buy the Elwha Dam and build its Washington Pulp and Paper Company, a pulp and paper mill at the foot of the Ediz Hook. It was a turning point not only for Aldwell, who went on to pursue other real estate and business interests, but for the peninsula. The pulp and paper industry ushered in a second wave of development that could put to use the region's vast hemlock forests, heretofore shunned as unsuitable for lumber production.

The second dam on the Elwha, Glines Canyon, was completed 8.6 miles upstream from the Elwha Dam in 1927 by Northwestern Power and Light Company—the successor to Aldwell's Olympic Power Company, in which he had since sold his interest—to fuel expansion of the Crown Zellerbach mill. The upper dam was connected to the Elwha Dam downriver by a remote-control system—and a hand-cranked telephone in an oak phone box. Surveying the site for the dam began in December 1925, with two engineers lowering themselves in bosun's chairs over the tearing torrent of the river to examine the river's canyon walls. Eventually rising 210 feet above the river, the dam was a simple, elegant structure.

Mills powered by Elwha Dam devoured virgin trees, such as this giant cedar, from the banks of the Elwha and surrounding forests. (Courtesy, Noreen Frink)

Both dams were part of the heyday of dam building in Washington, with Condit Dam completed on the White Salmon in 1913, Cushman No. 1 on the Skokomish in 1926, Diablo Dam under construction on the Skagit in 1917, and the series of dams up the Columbia River about to begin. In 1937 Crown Zellerbach Corporation (renamed in 1928) purchased Glines Canyon Dam, even as Bonneville Power Administration's regional power grid was rapidly under development. By 1949 the city of Port Angeles and Clallam County had turned to BPA for their power, leaving the dams with just one customer: the mill. It relied on the Elwha for 40 percent of its power, taking the rest from the grid.

The ease with which ecological and cultural considerations were pushed aside in the doing of all this are breathtaking today. In Port Angeles, as elsewhere, the march of industrialization was devastating to the natural environment and native

Work is underway in 1926 on Glines Canyon Dam, built to expand production at the Crown Zellerbach mill. The dam is now gone but the mill, under different ownership, still operates using power from the Bonneville power grid. (Courtesy, Nippon Paper Industries, Inc.)

Elk lost winter range habitat as the reservoirs were filled behind the Elwha dams. The stumps about to disappear underwater in this photo are visible again today. (Courtesy, Nippon Paper Industries, Inc.)

cultures. Both the lumber mill and pulp mill were built atop Tse-whit-zen, an ancient village of the Klallam people and a large burial ground. But the presence of the village site and sacred lands provoked even less concern than building two giant dams on the Elwha without fish passage. The territorial legislature protected fish runs—at least on paper. But developers of the mills faced no opposition as they pushed Indian ancestral bones out of the way and drove pilings straight through burial cairns. "Squatters and bones of Indians bother builders" was the headline in the *Crown Z News*, an internal company publication describing construction of the company's pulp mill on the Ediz Hook in 1920. In its April 1941 "Prosperity Edition" commemorating twenty years of progress on the Port Angeles waterfront, the *Port Angeles Evening News* featured in its full-page story on the mill a photograph of

human bones piled in a heap, a skull positioned upright on top to stare at the camera. The caption explained "some old Indian bones" were encountered while building the mill. The disturbance of an Indian burial ground did not even merit a story.

Busy developing nature for profit, industrialists overlooked (if they even noticed) the native people who had lived richly from the natural economy sustained by the Elwha and its watershed for thousands of years. The earliest use of the Tse-whit-zen site has been carbon dated to 2700 years ago. It was the largest of more than thirty-three villages of the Klallam people, stretching from the Hoko River to the shores of the Hamma Hamma and all the way across the Strait of Juan de Fuca into Canada. Klallam village sites and camps were also established up and down the Elwha River, far into the mountains. All were pushed aside by the newcomers as they settled and developed the river, the Ediz Hook, and the Port Angeles waterfront.

A period postcard of the Puget Sound Mills and Timber Company gives a sense of the fervor of industrialization transforming the town's waterfront and West End. The Big Mill—Puget Sound Mills and Timber Company—was loading its products on three and four steamers and sailing ships a day in the harbor. Later named the Charles Nelson Mill, it eventually was devouring five trains of ten cars each of logs daily. Merrill and Ring employed four hundred men in its mill and another two hundred felling timber in the woods. In 1924, 335 large oceangoing vessels called at Port Angeles to take shingles, lath, lumber, newsprint, and box board to all parts of the world.

But it was classic boom and bust. By 1930, the Charles Nelson Mill closed and its machinery was sold off. Merrill and Ring's plant on the same site shut down in 1988, after thirty

To Olympic Peninsula boosters of the early 1900s, the Elwha River was just waiting to be put to productive use. Here Kevin Yancy, the last manager of the Elwha dams, points out the soaring powerhouse at Elwha Dam in 2010.

years of operation. Crescent Boxboard, Fibreboard Products Corporation, PenPly Corporation, Olympic Forest Products, Rayonier Pulp and Paper, K-Ply Corporation—of more than a dozen major industrial facilities built on the West End, starting in 1914 with the Big Mill, all were shuttered eventually except for the pulp mill cranking out newsprint and paper for telephone directories, its scribble of steam rising at the base of the Ediz Hook. The latest incarnation of Crown Zellerbach's Washington Pulp and Paper Company, the mill (after many changes of ownership) celebrated its ninetieth anniversary

of operation in 2010. The mill in 2011 paid $27.91 an hour straight time, still some of the best money in Port Angeles—no matter that by then the company was owned by Nippon Paper Industries of Japan.

Yet a sense of the town's former industrial grandeur lived on in the dams. The Elwha Dam's powerhouse soared three stories high, its windows giving way to the sweep of the river just below. The powerhouse hummed and throbbed with the energy of the Elwha, the turbines and generators spinning gold from the river in the electricity that built the peninsula economy.

The beautiful black slate curvilinear control panel of Elwha Dam supported on steel Doric columns was a monument to the peninsula's industrial history now lost forever. During dam demolition, a few gauges were preserved, but the panel itself was destroyed.

Constructed during a grand industrial age in America, the mammoth works of the powerhouses were made of brass, steel, iron, and glass—and built to last. Both dams retained much of their original instrumentation to the end—though some of it, such as the hand-cranked telephone—had become merely decorative. But the main control panel of the dam, with its rows of dials and gauges set in panels of oil-black slate, supported by a curvilinear row of steel Doric columns, was still in use. Two of the turbines at the Elwha Dam were the oldest of their kind on the West Coast, spinning reliably to the last.

The dams' powerhouses were run by operators who knew by feel and experience when the machinery was running in its sweet spot—and when something was amiss. "It's mostly the vibrations and the smell; if you want to know the truth, I can feel this whole place breathing. It's alive," said operator Billy "Clutch" Cargo of Port Angeles. "Have you ever been a nanny?" Cargo asked me during a visit to the Elwha powerhouse one morning in September 2010. "When you sit here all day or night, it starts to become who you are. The solitude, the river—you can turn out the lights during the graveyard shift and feel that thrum at sixty cycles." Looking out the window of the powerhouse at the glass-green Elwha, he crossed his arms over his chest. "It's beautiful. I call this elephant grotto," he said, pointing to a pool of water right at the base of the dam, where the big fish still came back every August. "Right here, and they are huge," Cargo said. "You can't stand here and watch them bang their noses and not feel something; you got certain things on this planet that produce exceptionally large creatures, it's all right out there to see. The Elwha is a mythical river. The elk are huge. The trees are huge. The fish are huge."

Keeping the dams going year-round in mountain weather also took the work of men like Bob Williams of Port Angeles, who for forty years was part of a two-man maintenance crew taking care of both dams. Hydraulic mechanic, lineman, logger—whatever was needed, he did it. Back in the 1950s, Williams kept about 30 miles of transmission line cleared of fallen trees with a handsaw—or misery whip, as he called it—and cleaned carbon off the dams' generators by hand with a rag. "That was a nasty job," Williams said. "You get in there with rags and solvent and start mopping." Back in the day, he worked without earplugs, despite the generators' ninety-decibel roar. "You just sit there getting drilled in both ears." He knew the dark, cold parts of the canyons that the dams plugged, where the sun didn't climb high enough over the canyon walls to warm him until May and the wind came cutting off the lakes impounded by the dams. And he remembered the 1962 Columbus Day storm, when the wind blew so hard up the Elwha valley he saw a goose, trying to fly, pushed backward. ("Don't know whatever happened to that goose.") What he liked best of all was his independence, working at the remote dam site. "I didn't have nobody bugging me, I got to figure out what we were going to do that day, and there was always something to do."

I met Williams on a drippy, cold Saturday morning in May 2011 in Kevin Yancy's office. Manager of the Elwha Project for the Bureau of Reclamation, Yancy presided over the Elwha from a small office just east of the river, overlooking the Elwha Dam. His fishing rods and vest stood in one corner of the room, and pieces and parts of the dam that had been replaced over the years were stacked on shelves, relics from an era about to close. As we settled in for a talk in his office, Yancy called up Williams to come over and meet "the reporter lady from

Seattle." Williams, home cooking up elk steaks, obliged. "I hate to see it, myself," Williams said of the upcoming shutdown and dam removal as he sat reminiscing. "After so many years, it should be left alone, as far as I'm concerned."

Yancy walked me through the powerhouse with an oilcan and a soft cloth, polishing here, lubricating there. He had arrived at the Elwha Project in 2005 and found the dams in disrepair. With the dams slated to come out, maintenance had been neglected. He ordered up fresh paint, hung a new American flag snapping over the headgate house of the Glines Canyon Dam, and kept the old equipment humming. The grass outside was crew-cut short, and the brass and glass shone. I wanted to know how someone so obviously attached to the dams felt about their death-row status. I didn't have to ask twice. "Sometimes I would like to stand up and shout, 'Why are we doing this?' It doesn't make sense," Yancy said. "You look at how hard, what it took to put this in place, the lives lost; we are condemning that, and we are just going to take it down? It can get emotional real quick."

Spring ripened to the summer of 2011, the penultimate season for the dams. The Park Service started distributing sky-blue buttons in town with the slogan "Last Dam Summer" and offering public tours of the powerhouses. I decided to take a tour, mostly to see who showed up to say good-bye. An earnest-looking park ranger was passing out yellow hard hats and signing people up for the tour as I drove up to the dam. Waiting for the tour to get started, Dan Gouin of Port Angeles said he had his doubts about the so-called grand experiment about to begin. "I feel like it's a source of electricity that works, and who knows what will happen?" he said of the dams. "I don't know about restoring salmon,

and it won't be the same salmon. I'm always a person that hates change, and it's nice the lakes are there. It seems like a flaky, expensive thing to do. I'd just say no to salmon: it's not a vital food we need; it's a luxury. And there are so many other problems, so many factors."

Seeing Yancy, I bailed on the tour and went over to his office, surprised that he was there on a Saturday. With dam removal about to begin, he was in countdown mode, getting ready. His desk calendar had an unhappy face drawn on June 1, 2011: the date set for final shutdown of power generation at the dams. "It doesn't feel good," he said, sitting behind the too-tidy desk of a man who doesn't really use one. "We are cutting the heart out of these old girls. It's been a very tough deal; it's one of those things where we are doing what we have to do. This is my job. I am trying to be a good soldier, do what I was told to do. Some say, 'You are compromising your integrity, your character.' Well, somebody has to do it. Maybe the best one to do this dastardly, bastardly thing is me. And if it was any other river, I wouldn't do it. But the Elwha probably has the best potential." And then Yancy, a third-generation Bureau of Reclamation employee, said something that surprised me. Looking out the window of his office, where the Elwha died in Lake Aldwell, he said, "We can create more power plants. We can't re-create what the Creator did."

. . .

The day for shutdown broke gray and sullen. Yancy was wearing his best wool vest and a tie patterned with fishing flies for the occasion. He explained we'd go up to Glines first, shut down its generators, then come down to Elwha and switch it off too. He was matter of fact, a battlefield colonel pulling the troops from the field in a battle long over, decided somewhere else by people with a higher pay grade than his.

We caravanned behind his pickup to the Glines powerhouse, wondering what it would take to shut down a dam. Yancy swung open the door to the Glines powerhouse and walked to a control panel. The end, it turned out, was quick: a few throws of a switch, and the circuit was broken and the generators started to die. Yancy bent to a handwritten logbook and wrote "K. Yancy. On site to shut down Glines Canyon power plant, final day of operation. End of an era. Good-bye Glines!" He tied a red paper tag reading "Do Not Operate" to the control panel and headed for the door. "We're dead. That's it. She's done, buddy," Yancy said and piled into his truck.

In the powerhouse at Elwha Dam, he twirled knobs, pushed buttons, and finally pulled a large copper switch, as sparks jumped and sizzled. The lights abruptly went out. A battery-operated emergency light came on, giving the control room an intensive-care-unit glow. Yancy packed up his stuff to leave, gruff and not wanting to talk. "We've done the deed," he said. "Put her to bed. That's it. Show's over."

I walked out of the control room and stood by the generators, watching them twirl more and more slowly as they

Kevin Yancy pulls a final switch shutting down power at Elwha Dam after one hundred years of hydroelectric generation on June 1, 2011, in preparation for dam removal, marking the end of an era on the Elwha and the beginning of another.

Operator Billy "Clutch" Cargo leaves the Elwha Dam powerhouse for the last time, carrying the contents of his desk, including an old operator's manual and a can of spray cheese. Wrenches on a hand-made organizer hang behind the door.

gradually wound down, then finally stopped. Their heat was cooling, and the thrumming vibration of the room had stilled. With the power out, this industrial space was flooded with natural light from the floor-to-ceiling windows. And in this place that was always so loud that I screwed earplugs deep into my head anytime I was here, it was suddenly quiet. No, not quiet. There it was: the sound of the river.

Motion caught my eye. I looked up just in time to see Billy "Clutch" Cargo, the dam operator I'd met the previous summer, slipping out of the powerhouse; no one else recognized him. I darted after him; he had to be leaving the

powerhouse for the very last time. A couple of plastic grocery bags swung from his hands. Sure enough: the contents of his desk. A pair of dirty coveralls, an old operator's manual, a can of spray cheese, a couple of paperbacks from the grave-yard shift. Cargo's feet banged up the metal stairs leaving the powerhouse. He threw me a philosophical smile over his shoulder on the way out. "I'll find something," he said. "I'll go home and get the motor home ready. For the next job."

As he and Yancy were leaving, Robert Elofson, river restoration manager for the Lower Elwha Klallam Tribe; Brian Winter, head of the restoration effort for the National Park

Service; and some of the brass from Olympic National Park walked through the control room. "That's what I like," said Winter, looking at a gauge reading "Time Remaining: 00:00." They walked down the steps to the dead generators. It felt like a symbolic, if unofficial, changing of the guard. A bit of a quiet victory tour. It had taken a hundred years, but the hydro boys would never run this river again.

I asked Elofson what he was thinking. "I've got a few tears in my eyes," he said. "Tribal members always wanted the dams out of the river. The tribal councils, all of the natural resources people, my grandfather, all the people who fished the river when it was still healthy—they would be grateful. The saddest for me is that some of them aren't here any longer to see it."

Media, Park Service, congressional staff, and Lower Elwha Klallam tribal members witness generators gone still in the Elwha Dam powerhouse. For the first time in a century, the powerhouse went quiet but for the sound of the river.

A new world emerges as Lake Aldwell drains and the river cuts through a century of sediment. The orange color on the roots is caused by iron, newly exposed to air, precipitating out of formerly anoxic water in the lakebed.

4

RESTARTING THE CONVEYOR BELT

We heard the work underway before we saw it: the incongruous rumble and roar of steel-tracked heavy equipment with piercing backup alarms shattering the quiet in the wilderness of the park, 16 miles upriver above Lake Mills. Alder trees were yielding with a fatal, abrupt crack to the shove of a front-end loader. The operator loaded up the toppled trees and heaved them in dump trucks, stacking them like so much limp asparagus.

The construction of a pilot channel in the sediment delta at the upper end of Lake Mills was ordinary enough work in logging country but was extraordinary in this river setting in the middle of a federal wilderness area, signaling the start of big things to come. Completed in the fall of 2010, it was the very first step in the Elwha's recovery, opening a path for the river to follow as it cut its way through some 84 years of sediment supplied by the Elwha River.

The two dams on the Elwha had blocked the movement of much more than fish. They had also stopped the natural flow of cobbles, gravel, silt, and logs a river continually carries from the mountains all the way down its length. Taking the dams out wasn't only about letting fish come back up the river, it was also about letting all that material come back down. But just how to manage decades' worth of that material piled up behind the dams as they were taken out was one of the most vexing problems in the project. Some 24 million cubic yards of sediment, gradually trapped by the dams, would have to be slowly, carefully released. It would be the largest controlled release of sediment, many times over, ever attempted in a dam removal, and it would influence the pace and method of dam removal on the Elwha—and define many of the project's risks.

In 2010, contractors for the National Park Service dig a pilot channel through a giant delta of sediment built up behind Glines Canyon Dam and grown over with an alder forest.

HOW MUCH IS **24 MILLION** CUBIC YARDS?

One of the biggest tasks in Elwha Dam removal was managing the controlled release of about 24 million cubic yards of sediment trapped behind it and Glines Canyon Dam. The plan was to let the river do the work, gradually rinsing the material downstream and redistributing it. Taking it away with excavators and trucks was determined to be too expensive and would generate too much truck traffic.

24 million cubic yards = 72,072 mining-truck loads

6-foot person

The CAT 797B mining truck can carry 333 cubic yards per load.

🚚 = 100 loads

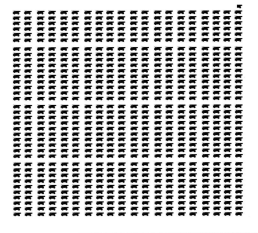

24 million cubic yards = 8 Safeco Fields filled to the top of the retractable roof

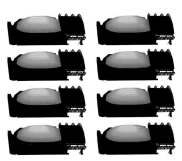

Sources: NBBJ, architecture and design firm; Caterpillar Company

MARK NOWLIN and AMANDA RAYMOND / THE SEATTLE TIMES

The Elwha delivered an estimated 400,000 cubic yards of sediment every year to the upper reservoir behind the Glines Canyon Dam in a long-term average from 1927 to 2010, according to calculations by the US Bureau of Reclamation. But instead of the material rinsing downriver to the sea, it formed a vast delta of silt, cobble, sand, gravel, and boulders behind both dams. Restarting the river's capacity to transport that material is one of the most important elements in the restoration of the Elwha. Especially in the Olympics, rivers naturally move not only mountains of sediment and rock, but wood too. Not just sticks, but giant root wads, gnarly hunks of broken branches, and entire trees felled as rivers restlessly migrate across their floodplains and chew their banks.

Queets, Hoh, Elwha: these are fierce mountain rivers, growling with mighty appetites, requiring a steady diet of wood and rock from their watersheds. They are the square meals a healthy river eats every day to build the bones of its bed, its channels, its gravel bars and riffles. And a river is always busy: Building massive logjams and tearing them apart. Carving side channels, then meandering away from them to wander somewhere else. Digging pools. Mounding gravel. Tumbling cobble and, in big storms, rolling boulders. Healthy rivers are never-ending construction zones, powered by the forces of gravity and gradient, as well as the solar energy of the water cycle that delivers the rain and snow that keeps it all going. Primal, eternal, it's a process of destruction and renewal relentless enough to nag mountains all the way down to sand in the bottom of the sea. It just takes a while.

But on the Elwha, the dams had stopped the perpetual motion of the river and shut down its conveyor belt, starving everything below the dams for the building material the river naturally delivers. You can see the results. Above the dams, the river's form is beautifully complex, with its battlements of logjams, gravel bars, plunge pools, and side channels. In between and below the dams lies the land of less: Less gravel. Less complexity of form. Less diversity of habitat. Less life.

Restarting the conveyor belt of the river, with so much sediment now trapped behind the dams, would not be simple. Instead of a nice, big, cathartic blow and go, managers would have to take the dams down gradually, to release the piled-up sediment slowly and safely. Leaving a natural-looking landscape behind rather than a moonscape of sediment cliffs is another big challenge of the Elwha dam removal project. It is a high-stakes, real-time science project like none other. More than seven hundred dams had been removed around the nation by the time the Elwha's turn came, but in terms of the amount of sediment released, they were all much smaller projects, not even remotely on this scale.

Dredging and slurrying the sediment out to the Strait of Juan de Fuca at a cost of some $22 million was rejected as impractical during the environmental impact analysis of the project. The river was going to have to do the work on its own. The problem, though, was not allowing the river to slice through the sediment too quickly. Just let the river go, and it would bore right through the soft, unconsolidated material, leaving unnatural, unstable cliffs behind to totter and fall. That was unacceptable in a national park and potentially dangerous.

Instead, scientists wanted the river to meander back and forth across the face of the sediment deltas piled up behind the dams, sluicing out the material like a moving fire hose. A lot of the sediment would still be left behind—probably about half. The goal was to get the river to shape it in stepped-down

TAKING DOWN THE ELWHA RIVER DAMS

Different methods were used to remove the Elwha and Glines Canyon dams on the Elwha River in stages, beginning in September 2011. Dam removal was paused along the way to make the process safer and easier on fish in the river.

GLINES CANYON DAM

A The level of Lake Mills is lowered 17 feet to the bottom of the spill gates.

B The first 17 feet of the dam are removed down to the new water level.

C The next 173 feet of the dam are removed by taking out notches on alternating sides. The headgate house, penstock (pipe used to carry water to the powerhouse) and the powerhouse are removed.

NOTE: The only remaining structures will be the spillway and the thrust block (a massive, reinforced block of concrete), which will become viewing platforms with interpretive signs about the restoration project.

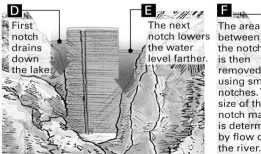

D First notch drains down the lake.

E The next notch lowers the water level farther.

F The area between the notches is then removed by using smaller notches. The size of the notch made is determined by flow of the river.

G The process continues down to the lowest layer.

H Once the lowest layer is removed, the river channel will be restored.

ELWHA DAM

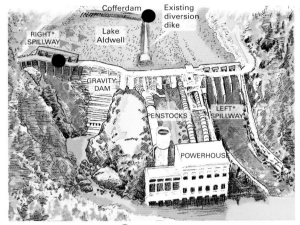

After Lake Aldwell is lowered 15 feet (to the bottom of the spillway gates) by releasing water through the left and right spillways, a cofferdam is built in front of the right spillway.

The right spillway concrete is removed.

The cofferdam is removed. The water level is dropped, drying the left forebay.

The left spillway is removed and a section of bedrock is blasted out. The river flows out the resulting channel.

The dam's middle section is removed, then the penstocks (pipes used to carry water to the powerhouse) are removed.

The original river channel is excavated, requiring the removal of 200,000 cubic yards of fill (fir trees, rock, earth, and concrete) from behind the gravity dam. The gravity dam is removed.

The powerhouse is removed and the area is restored to a more natural terrain.

The diversion channel is filled in and the Elwha River flows into the opened original channel.

* Right and left labels are in accordance with looking downstream, from behind the dam.

Sources: Olympic National Park Public Affairs Office, interactive-earth.com

MARK NOWLIN / THE SEATTLE TIMES

Scientists gather on a bluff above the Elwha River in the summer of 2010 to discuss research possibilities. The potential to learn about restoration at the watershed scale is one of the most exciting aspects of the Elwha project.

terraces, built with each stage of lowering the river. Notching the dams gradually and waiting as much as two weeks between drops in gradient would control the pace of the river's work. That was the plan, anyway. Scientists had built lots of computer models, and even 3-D simulations of how the river would behave as the dams came down. But what would really happen?

"I've looked at the pictures, I've been to the talks," said Gordon Grant, research hydrologist with the US Department of Agriculture's Pacific Northwest Research Station in Corvallis, Oregon. "What we put together in the lab was not nature. It's almost time to watch this thing come out. And it's going to be both more and less exciting than people think." There would be wild cards, for sure, he added: Buried stumps 6 feet across. Standing forests long lost under sediment trapped at the end of Lake Mills by the Glines Canyon Dam. The upper dam of the two, it had been hoarding sediment for eighty-four years by 2011. "Who knows what we will find?" Grant said. "Probably Jimmy Hoffa, too."

Tim Randle, manager of the Sedimentation and River Hydraulics Group in the Technical Service Center of the Bureau of Reclamation, located at the bureau's Denver office, led management of the sediment for the Elwha restoration project. Together with Jennifer Bountry, a hydraulic engineer also in the Sedimentation and River Hydraulics Group, they jokingly referred to themselves as Team Delta Force "because we are trying to get the delta to do what we want," Bountry said. "You kind of have a tiger by the tail," Randle told the scientists. "And the only knob you can turn is how quickly you take the dams down."

Removal of the dams was planned to be held at 1.5 feet per stage, he said, with recovery time between stages to let the river settle down. There would be stops in the action altogether for as much as half the year, too. That was to protect fish in the lower river that heavy sediment loads were expected to kill. It was also important to go slowly to avoid raising the risk of flooding posed by letting the riverbed build up too much too quickly.

To probe the river's transport capacity and dynamics, researchers embedded microchips in numbered river cobbles and tossed them back in the river, to enable long-term monitoring of the rocks' movement using a radio antenna.

Anna Torrance of the National Park Service helps shovel river cobble on a bar during an exploration of the river's movement during gradual drawdown of both reservoirs prior to dam removal.

But before starting dam removal in September 2011, one of the first problems to solve was what to do about the sediment delta built up behind the upper dam. Piled deep at the upper end of Lake Mills, it had been here so long that it was grown over thickly with an alder forest. The Elwha was being held up here—perched—by about 20 million cubic yards of muck piled up and rooted in place, shoving the river to the side of its east channel—exactly what Team Delta Force, counting on the river to sweep back and forth across the delta to rinse out the sediment, didn't want.

Would a nice big storm in the winter of 2010–11 set up the river in a better spot, more toward the middle of the channel? The Elwha had a well-known potential for roughhouse. Logjams two stories high, seemingly so permanent, could just as easily be gone after the next winter storm. Maybe the river would take care of things by itself. But could the team afford to chance just leaving it be? What would they do if that didn't work?

Randle had been visiting the Elwha in preparation for dam removal since 1994. Typical of a new generation of scientists and engineers at state, federal, and tribal resource agencies, his career wasn't about building new infrastructure today so much as altering it or even taking it out, to meet changing environmental and economic realities. The Elwha was his biggest challenge yet in a rapidly evolving field still defining the state of its art—drawing scientists from around the country to investigate the Elwha's potential for research problems. "This was a debate," Randle said. "Should we just let it unfold and see what happens? If you had the ability to easily try something that might be an option but your ability to do anything different is really limited if it doesn't work, you are in a risk management calculation. You might get lucky and avoid expense, but if you don't and it doesn't work, you would really wish you had [intervened]. You could have a lot of trouble later; if you had to get equipment out there, there would be no way to barge it anymore—you'd have to build some kind of road, and then how would you unload it? Helicopters are a lot of expense, and there is the marbled murrelet [to consider] and working in a federal wilderness area. You are talking about brigades with fire hoses."

Excavating the pilot channel we witnessed under construction was the $743,708 solution. In the fall of 2010, contractors carved a 1100-foot-long, 50-foot-wide, 6-foot-deep trench down the middle of the sediment delta; cut down the alder forest; and moved a giant logjam piece by piece, repositioning it to divert the river into the engineered slot. But the question was, what would happen next, over winter, in the rumpus room of the upper reaches of the Elwha, still never collared by dams?

. . .

Federal contractors felled the alder forest grown up on the sediment delta behind Glines Canyon Dam and dug a pilot channel down the middle in preparation for dam removal. (Tom Roorda)

I was surprised when we came back again the next spring to see just how much it all had changed. Randle and Bountry came out from Denver to investigate as soon as the weather settled down in May 2011. We had hiked down the same fishermen's trail when it was ablaze in late summer light on our last visit, and now native plants were in their spring glory. Dogtooth violets with their delicate yellow faces glinted along the path, purple orchids glowed, and the gleaming white of trillium, with its powdered gold stamens, lifted bright above the ferns. Trout lily was the standout, though, with its spotted leaves and the dainty perfection of its nodding white blossom.

We edged onto the delta, surprising a deer. We couldn't believe we were standing in the same place where we'd been last fall. The logs we had sat on were all gone, and of course the alders were too. The tidy, straight-sided, engineered channel we'd seen was also gone, replaced by a natural meander as the Elwha chewed back and forth across the delta—just as Randle had hoped.

"We are starting off with perfect conditions here," he said, looking cheered by the payoff on an expensive gamble with taxpayers' money. Now he hoped that as the dams started to come out, the river's own energy would get to work, rolling

US Bureau of Reclamation researchers used this device towed behind a kayak to help detect the shape and calculate the volume of sediment piled up behind Glines Canyon Dam prior to dam removal.

Joshua Chenoweth of the National Park Service walks along deep terraces of sediment piled on the former bed of Lake Mills in spring 2012. The remains of Glines Canyon Dam and the lake are visible in the far distance behind him.

What to do with some 24 million cubic yards of sediment stuck behind the dams? Managers looked at trucking and dredging it out but decided to let the river erode much of it, with about half left behind in terraces along the banks.

With the beginning of reservoir drawdown in summer of 2011, before dam removal began, the transformation of the landscape above the dams was already underway. These trees bear witness to the prior water level in Lake Aldwell.

cobbles in the muck and exposing fine sediments that would sluice downriver. "With rivers, slope is everything; the delta doesn't belong here, and the river is going to take it away. It's all about gradient," Randle said. Gradient would be created first by reservoir drawdown, then dam removal. Taking out the structures, chunk by chunk, and dropping the water level would set the river loose to do its work.

We reached the delta and started walking around. Roots from the alders that had been knocked over the previous fall stuck out of the sediment flats like broken wire. The delta was

a moonscape of tire tracks from heavy equipment. It was hard to envision restoration of this mess.

We came back again in July 2011 to have another look after Yancy had shut down power generation at the dams. When we arrived at the same boat ramp we had used to take out our raft after our float trip the previous spring, we discovered the ramp dangling 14 feet above the river's surface. Trees along what had been the waterline suddenly looked oddly sheared, the straight line of the previous water level trimming them as evenly as a barber might, like bangs cut too high up the forehead. Between

Thick layers of sediment engulf a giant stump exposed in the former bed of Lake Aldwell in the spring of 2012. The author is 5 feet 9 inches and the stump and sediment layers are quite a bit taller.

the ramp to nowhere and the water's distant edge was a vast beach of sediment, with the river running through it where before had been a lake. It was a transforming landscape. Dam removal had yet to begin, but just by lowering the reservoirs some 15 to 17 feet in preparation for demolition, the river already was coming back to life.

We gathered our gear and headed out onto the delta, hopping down from the ledge that so recently had been the water's edge. Giant cedar stumps left from when the forest was logged, back before the reservoirs were flooded, studded

the beach. "Careful, it can be just like quicksand," Randle said, taking the lead. Joining him to check on progress of the project was fluvial geomorphologist Brian Cluer, in the habitat conservation office of the National Marine Fisheries Service's Southwest regional office in Santa Rosa, California. Like many, he had worked on the Elwha for years and was finally getting his first look at the river's ongoing transformation.

We walked across a broad expanse of sediment where there had been a lake just three months ago. Cluer noticed it first: the sound of the river, where it hadn't been heard for a hundred

Here, just days after the Elwha Dam was completely removed in March, 2012, the river tore through the former bed of Lake Aldwell.

years. "First the sound," Cluer said, "then the salmon." And, eventually, so many other animals, he hoped. He remembered camping in the upper reaches of the Elwha years before and seeing a bear come down to the river's edge with great purpose, look around, and then leave. Salmon, Cluer figured, was what it was looking for. "I felt so sorry for that bear," Cluer said. "I'm doing this partly for him." I looked at Cluer closely and was pretty sure he wasn't kidding. I wasn't surprised. A lot of the experts working year in and out on the Elwha felt their work was more than just a job or a technical exercise. "This is something I've wanted to do my whole career: to come back here and follow this through. I've been on dam removals, but this is the first big one," Cluer said. "It's exciting to come home to the Elwha and see it get reborn. I think it will happen fast; I want to see what is up here in twenty, thirty years."

As we walked the delta, we kept finding what the reservoirs left behind as they drained: a beaver jaw, a woman's high buttoned shoe, a soda can from back when they were made of steel and had flat bottoms. One day, this land would be a forest, like it used to be. For now, just a few grasses struggled out of the ashen sediment flats; I was surprised to see anything growing there at all. It was so easy to forget that this was a true

Replanting nearly 800 acres of sediment left behind after the reservoirs drained is an unprecedented challenge. This sample of sediment looks more like roadbed material than anything plants would ever grow in.

watershed restoration, not just a river project. But the sediment flats were a good reminder of that, crisscrossed as they were with animal tracks. Elk, raccoons, and herons had all been here, investigating the emerging landscape. In a pocket formed in the sediment, a plant with a tiny white flower had taken hold. The river ran topaz blue and teal, luminous against the gray banks.

The Mount St. Helens eruption of May 18, 1980, in some ways was nothing compared with the challenge of revegetating some 800 acres of this stuff. While St. Helens was a much bigger disturbance, at least there was soil left behind after the mighty volcano blew, from which new life could spring. Revegetation of the former lake beds exposed when the reservoirs behind the dams drop is in some respects more challenging. It's not like regeneration after a fire or blowdown; it's more like starting over after the retreat of a glacier. Just how the landscape grows in—whether by invasive weeds or desirable native plants—will be the single most visible piece of the Elwha restoration effort. "It gets overlooked, but it is what everyone is going to see," said Joshua Chenoweth, botanical restorationist at Olympic National Park who is helping to lead the revegetation effort for the National Park Service.

Beyond appearance, replanting is necessary in some areas too far from natural seed sources for nature to do the work. Because, for fish restoration to succeed, the landscape must be restored to a healthy, functioning native forest. Upland forests are intimately linked to the health of the rivers that run through them. Forests provide the rain of nutritious litter that falls into the river, feeding bugs and other invertebrates that are the base of the aquatic food chain. Upland trees, shrubs, and plants also hold the soil, prevent erosion, and shade and

David Allen, botanist for the National Park Service, surveys transplants destined for the Elwha. The seven-year planting program is challenged by inhospitable ground, including areas of powdery fine material, with no soil, as much as 5 feet thick.

cool the water. And when it falls into the river, woody debris provides the complexity in the river channel that lets the river create scours, pools, and side channels. The river's perpetual tumble cycle also sorts and distributes the cobble and gravel the fish need to build their nests. So desperate had the shortage of this gravel become in the lower river because of the dams that fish aficionados for years resorted to rolling boulders by hand, to expose the gravel fish need.

All that sediment trapped above the dams posed another problem as well. Once the dams were out, the unnaturally thick deposition of fine material—5 feet and more deep—was going to make regrowth of a healthy, native landscape very challenging. So inhospitable are the fine sediments to plant growth that even Himalayan blackberry, a notorious invader, would not grow in some test plots. "It's not often you see 1 to 5 feet of fines," Chenoweth said. "We know things will grow [in it], native grasses for sure." But what's really needed are woody shrubs that hold the ground, so the revegetation team would

Joshua Chenoweth surveys new transplants, just a few of more than 400,000 native plants and 5000 pounds of seed gathered from the Elwha watershed that will be planted in the former lake beds in a bid to out-compete invasive weeds.

plant those abundantly. The soils aren't that bad everywhere, and within 160 feet of the forest growing along the former reservoir banks, nature is expected to revegetate the land unassisted. But elsewhere, the project lands would be actively reseeded and replanted.

The Lower Elwha Klallam Tribe back in 2002 began cutting, spraying, and pulling weeds that would otherwise be the seed source for an invasion of exotic plants. But by the summer of 2012, weeds were already crowding into the former Lake Aldwell, including reed canary grass, orchard grass, and Scotch broom. But there was good news too: cottonwoods had heavily seeded the receding lakeshore as it dropped during the 2011 drawdown, and a legacy of wetland plants along the former shoreline were surviving in the still-moist sediments. Spores also had grown into a verdant rug of mosses that was helping to trap moisture and provide a place for seeds to lodge and sprout. Cracks that opened in the drying sediment were, surprisingly, proving an important asset, helping with gas exchange in the tight substrate and providing shaded, moist environments where plants and mosses were thriving.

The unprecedented replanting effort in the Elwha is full of surprises, such as the lush growth of moss on the former lakebeds. A big help, the moss retains moisture and provides a place where seeds can catch hold and sprout.

Gathering seeds from native plants in the Elwha ensured that plants used in the restoration are suited to the watershed. In the first round of replanting, Chenoweth and volunteers planted more than forty-nine species.

And since 2001, the forest that scientists hope will one day grow on this land has also been quietly in the works, growing from seeds gathered by hand from the Elwha watershed to be broadcast on the project lands. David Allen, Park Service botanist, has overseen the growth of tens of thousands of plants that he hopes will become established in the project lands in a seven-year revegetation plan with planting begun in the winter of 2011–12. More than 400,000 plants and more than 5000 pounds of seed will eventually be planted to revegetate the landscape. The revegetation project, which continues until 2017, is unprecedented in its scale; most of what's

being attempted here would require adaptation of the plan as it unfolded, Allen said. "We can't go into this with the idea that we know everything," Allen said. "We will have to adapt, find what works." By the spring of 2012, the riverbanks and terraces of sediment were studded with new growth; the question was how long the brave seedlings and planted material would live as summer heated up.

. . .

The river also had a lot of work ahead of it, rebooting its transport function. There was enough material trapped behind these dams to affect the function of the entire ecosystem below them. With sediment yields to the delta reduced, the beach at the river's mouth was eroded in some places by the waves to ankle-turning cobble. It wasn't only the fault of the dams. A water-supply pipeline built by the city of Port Angeles at the foot of sea cliffs west of the city had walled off the bluffs above the coast, reducing their natural nourishment of the beach. The two alterations may have also contributed to the natural instability of the Ediz Hook east of the river. The US Army Corps of Engineers had been stepping up its efforts at a cost of about $100,000 a year to artificially maintain the spit, which extends some 3.5 miles into the Strait of Juan de Fuca and supports the only access road to a major US Coast Guard air and sea rescue station. A storm in the winter of 1974–75 spurred a rescue effort by the corps, which installed a $6 million pile of rocks the length of the west side of the hook that has needed maintenance ever since, just to keep salt water from breaching the spit.

Visitors to the hook today must first drive through the guts of the Nippon Paper Industries mill, a bizarre and uninviting

In their diversity of color and form, seeds of native plants create a tapestry of elegant beauty. Volunteers gathered, sorted, and dried seeds of native grasses, flowers, woody shrubs, and trees from the Elwha watershed for the replanting effort.

Scientist Ian Miller of Washington Sea Grant surveys cobble on the beach at the river mouth. In the summer of 2012 he spotted the first accretion of sand on the eroding beach he could attribute to dam removal.

experience that feels like trespassing, to reach what's left of the hook. Boulders are piled so high on its north side, the view from a car is of a forbidding wall that blocks any glimpse of the water. There's no beach on that side to walk, enjoy, or even see at all. On the south side, there's a bit of grass, a few park benches, and a narrow strip of beach. It's a good place to stand and look back at the city of Port Angeles toward the Olympics, where the snows feed the river that drove the dams, that blocked the sediment and killed the fish, that powered the mill that displaced the tribe. It is easy to see, in one industrial sacrifice zone, how all the pieces of natural and human history are connected and how much one place gave, lost, and gained in pursuit of "progress."

For the Lower Elwha Klallam Tribe, the assault of erosion on the shoreline was personal. Hunks of their reservation have washed away year by year. Jonathan Warrick, a research geologist at the USGS Pacific Coastal and Marine Science Center in Santa Cruz, California, documented 22 acres lost along the Elwha River delta since 1939 due to coastal erosion, and also found the rate of erosion is increasing. On the tribe's reservation, the changes are the most dramatic, with total erosion averaging 125 feet between 1939 and 2006 and some spots chewed back as much as 500 feet. No wonder tribal members talk of running cattle with their grandparents on pastures that are simply gone today. A whole way of life was lost at The Place near the river's mouth, as it was called, where in the 1900s tribal members had enjoyed swimming holes that no longer exist and gathered shellfish from beaches no longer there. Bea Charles, born in 1919, used to talk about savoring the clams her family collected, particularly after a storm, when the family would take their baskets down to pick up shellfish thrown up on the soft sand. Her aunt, Adeline, ninety-three in 2011, remembered the string of butter clams that her mother kept behind the stove for snacking. Those beaches are gone today.

Al Charles Sr., another Klallam elder on the reservation, remembered watching for gulls wheeling in the sky by the hundreds after a big wind. "We knew as soon as we saw that, there was plenty of clams at the mouth of the river; we would run down with our baskets and buckets. And a beautiful sandbar there, with plenty of flounder. We used to catch them right off the beach. And halibut so big they ran the . . . [length] of the canoe. We used to have fun on that old river mouth in the cedar dugout of my dad's; we'd go shooting out on the swift water." Today the flounders were gone, Charles said, and the clams, along with the soft, sandy beach he remembered from when he was seven years old. Now there were just cobbles and rock, no sand at all. "There is nothing coming down the Elwha anymore," Charles said. "It's all behind the dams."

Elwha chinook return for their fall run to their hereditary spawning grounds, only to be blocked by Elwha Dam just 5 miles from the river mouth. Even after a century of futility the fish never stopped trying to come home.

5
THE HOUSE
OF TYEE

It was late summer 2010, and the Elwha River was so low, there was just enough water leaking through the Elwha Dam to fill a pool right at its base. Big boulders exposed by low water invited our passage to a rocky outcropping with a perfect view into the pool. We hiked over and scrambled up the rocks for a look. And there they were. Elwha chinook, returned for their futile fall run, trying to reach the spawning grounds above the dams that still called them, even after a hundred years.

They were blocked at the dam just 5 miles from the river mouth. Some circled in the pool. Some hung still in the water, right in a row, actually facing the dam as if to stare it down by sheer will. I couldn't believe that they were there at all, these fish about which I had heard so much but never seen alive, swimming in the river as adults. Still genetically distinct from any other salmon in Puget Sound, still the kings of them all, these were the *tyee* capable of growing to spectacular size, staying out in the open ocean as long as seven years. They were made to master this mountain river, with bodies that could, if conditions were right, grow big enough to thrash all the way to the top of the watershed.

If Elwha River recovery has an icon, it is this fish. Bringing back the Elwha River kings has been a rallying cry for advocates of dam removal for more than a generation. Even today, after being raised since the 1970s primarily in hatchery trays and a concrete rearing channel run by the state of Washington, these chinook still grow to monster size. As we watched them idle in the pool, just downstream more fish were still coming. Every now and then, one would break the surface in a long arc just below the windows of the powerhouse, its splash punctuating the mechanical drone of the generators.

The Elwha was once home to ten runs of native, ocean-going salmon and trout, including all five species of Pacific salmon: chinook, chum, coho, pink, sockeye. There was no month of the year in which the Elwha River was not alive with fish, either migrating upstream, spawning, rearing, or beginning their journey as juveniles to the great pastures of the sea. The river's early abundance was something no one thought to measure. Lower Elwha Klallam tribal members say pinks used to swarm the river, so many fish filling the river they startled

horses. They talk of their elders using wheelbarrows to bring home their catch. Elder Adeline Smith remembers one year when she was fishing, the salmon she caught was so big, she straddled the fishing pole as two men helped her bring it in.

Elwha fish stories have been part of the Northwest's cultural fabric as long as people have been fishing and living here. There was a time when a photo of someone in the family tree posing with one of these fish was virtually a Northwest birthright. William Roy Clark, of Maple Valley, Washington, remembers the photos taken by his grandfather, Frank Clark, the first powerhouse operator at the Elwha Dam, of the fish killed while blasting the spillway at the bottom of the dam. "One that made a huge impression on me and my sisters showed a chinook that hung from the front porch beam of the big house on the road down at the dam, and its nose touched the second step down," he said. "That fish had to weigh 110 pounds." Fish killed by blasting were used to feed the dam construction crews. Later, once the dam was in and his grandfather at the helm, "Whenever Grandma wanted salmon for dinner, she would go down and tell him to shut off the powerhouse," Clark said. One quick snag into the same pool we were looking at, and there was dinner.

▪ ▪ ▪

The Treaty of Point No Point, signed by the Klallam people in 1855, was supposed to relocate the Lower Elwha Klallam Tribe to the Skokomish Reservation, at the southern end of the long arm of Hood Canal. That was nowhere near their home, with their ancestral lands, homes, burial places, and fishing, gathering, and hunting grounds. Most never left and instead clung to their place here, eventually receiving a small reservation in

Mike McHenry, habitat biologist for the Lower Elwha Klallam Tribe (left) and Ernest "Sonny" Sampson III, senior fisheries technician, watch king salmon circle beneath Elwha Dam. Both fought for decades to keep the fish alive, while pushing for dam removal.

1968, just 372 acres. The federal government bought the land in 1936 but delayed more than thirty years putting it into trust for the tribe, in part because of local opposition by sport fishermen.

Once the largest and most powerful tribe on the Olympic Peninsula, the number of Klallam people had shrunk to only 485 tribal members by the time of the 1880 census—the result of epidemics. Smallpox and other diseases ravaged the native people following the arrival of Spanish explorers. The outbreak of infectious diseases began in about the 1770s on the Northwest Coast, maybe earlier, killing an estimated 80 percent of the coastal Indians in the first century of contact. In Port Angeles, the survivors were pushed off what had been their traditional village sites along the waterfront during the time of white settlement beginning in about the 1850s.

Prior to building the dams on the river, the Klallams fished Elwha River salmon stocks in the Strait of Juan de Fuca, at the mouth of the Elwha, in the river's lower reaches, and at Indian Creek, a tributary of the Elwha where the tribe also had a permanent village site, and other small streams that are part of the Elwha River system. Even as the new town of Port Angeles began to take shape around them in the 1890s, the Elwha people still supported themselves from subsistence fisheries and by selling fish to the townspeople. But with the damming of the river beginning in 1910, that changed, as state game wardens pursued, arrested, jailed, and fined tribal fishermen for catching fish in the river that bore their name—a violent, systematic violation of tribal members' treaty right to fish.

By the winter of 1935, when federal land agents appraised the farms in the lower Elwha valley for the purpose of acquiring 3840 acres of land for the tribe for a reservation, George G. Wren, assistant land negotiator for the federal government, had the following to report of the living conditions endured by the parents and grandparents of many of the tribal members living at Lower Elwha today:

The Indians depended largely upon beachcombing for their living. In bygone years, salmon, trout, crab, and other fishing and clam digging activities furnished a means of livelihood for most of the Indians of the area. However, the Indians cannot compete with the large fishing industries now established. The Washington State Fish and Game Laws now prevent the Indians from catching enough fish for their own use as food. When an Indian is caught fishing out of season, he is given the choice of either a jail sentence or a fine. Out of necessity, his choice is invariably a jail sentence.

A dam on the Elwha River, owned and maintained by a pulp company, has ruined the spawning grounds of the trout and salmon. The opening of this dam several times each year results in killing thousands of fish. The Indians gather the dead fish in order to replenish their food supply. However, the president of the Klallam Indian Tribal Council informed the writer that even the possession of fish thus killed has, in several instances, resulted in jail sentences for the possessor.

Tribal member Mel Elofson, on the tribe's fishery staff since 1993, remembered what that used to be like, writing in his memoirs:

Gordon Sampson had taken my brother and me to . . . snag salmon from the riverbank, for one of our first trips to the river. We were probably about twelve years old then. We were scared because our cousin Gordon had said that what we were going to do was illegal and to run and hide if we saw a fisheries enforcement officer. This was also fun because we

Reservoirs heated by a 1987 drought spiked a once rare disease in Elwha River chinook, killing more than 2000 fish in the lower river. A state fisheries worker stacks a frozen 50-pound chinook among the dead. (Natalie Fobes, *Seattle Times*, 1987)

were good at hide and seek. On future trips we were always sneaking up . . . to capture as many fish as we were able to carry or drag back home. . . . There were many who counted on salmon as food and a way to make some cash to buy other needs.

It wasn't until the US District Court's 1974 decision by Judge George Boldt that tribal members could finally fish without harassment, a right their ancestors had reserved for the tribe in perpetuity under the 1855 treaty, in return for cession of their lands to the United States. Judge Boldt's decision, nearly 120 years after their ancestors signed the treaty, finally provided a critical means for tribal members to survive as Indian people

in a changing world, as their ancestors had hoped. For Indian people, Boldt's decision was life-changing. Elofson's memoir continues:

We fished the Elwha illegally until the Judge Boldt decision, which changed forever the way the tribes could fish for salmon. There was no more sneaking around the river or having confrontations with state fisheries enforcement; many of us were elated that we could finally make a living and feed families without interference. I myself spent many years on the river making a comfortable living as a young teen to a grown adult. In my late twenties to mid-thirties, I and my brother bought a small trawler where we fished the Strait of Juan de Fuca for black mouth and coho. I also participated as a deckhand fishing large gillnet boats for several summers.

The treaty-protected fishery remains a cultural touchstone and, in good years, an important economic opportunity, especially in other parts of the tribe's traditional fishing area, including the Strait of Juan de Fuca and around the San Juan Islands, where tribal members go out for sockeye, halibut, crab, and more.

But on their home river, the tribe's treaty right is frustrated by a habitat so degraded by the dams that it produces few fish. In a river that used to see at least 390,000 fish a year come back, in the Elwha today sockeye are long extinct, pinks are nearly gone, and steelhead, chinook, bull trout, and eulachon are threatened with extinction and listed for protection under the Endangered Species Act. Hatchery coho and steelhead provide a little fishing opportunity in the lower river, but nothing to live on. The chinook catch is limited to just a few fish a year, strictly for ceremonial use.

The Klallam people for generations were forced to watch the river slowly decline, like a family member on life support, while the state and federal agencies charged with honoring their treaty rights mostly just stood by and watched. Elofson also wrote in his memoirs of his grandmother's homestead along the river, near the Elwha Dam, where she would walk in the late summer to see the same pool at the base of the dam that we had, to watch the fish:

When I was a young teenager in 1970 and 1971, I spent a lot of time with my grandmother Louisa Sampson. She had many stories that she was always proud to tell me. She had spoken of salmon on the Elwha River that were so thick a person could walk from one bank to the other across their

backs. . . . She said she was devastated to see so many thousands of salmon dying at the base of the dam; because there was no other passage for them to move further upstream, many went unspawned and she said she was quite distressed from this experience. All she could do was go back home, and (she) said she cried for hours.

In September 2010, we saw about twenty-two adult fish in that same pool, descendants, genetically, of Grandmother Louisa's fish. Only about five hundred in all came back to the river in 2010, a record low.

The dams harmed not only adult fish trying to migrate upriver, but juveniles stranded below the dams by the thousands, as dam managers ramped the river's flow up and down to meet their power needs. Elders in the Lower Elwha Klallam Tribe today still talk of running with buckets to rescue flipping shoals of silvery fish stranded at the river's edge, scooping them from puddles to put them back in the river. Poachers and even live powerlines dropped in the river also exterminated fish. Habitat was unsuitable below the dams—from lack of good spawning gravel and fewer pools, side channels, and riffles. Some years, the water below the lower dam became so warm because of the river's plugged flow, fish biologists launched an emergency evacuation, netting every adult fish returning to the river and spawning it artificially, for fear of otherwise losing the entire run. In 1987, thousands of adult chinook were lost to disease incubated by warm reservoir discharge.

. . .

As the afternoon sun swung across the canyon, it lit the pool below the dam even more brightly. The fish shone, brilliant in their silver jackets. Steve shot photo after photo in the perfect, penetrating light, video too, to capture the fish trying over and over to swim where they could not go.

We headed next to the state's fish weir, downstream. Temporarily erected right in the river like a fence, the weir was being used to sample adult fish coming upstream. Caught in a metal trap at one end, fish made a racket, banging a gate in the trap until they were released. As we arrived we could hear a fish slamming away in the trap from way up the hill. We followed the sound down to the weir to meet Kent Mayer, a biologist with the Washington Department of Fish and Wildlife, checking the trap to see what the weir had caught overnight. We hoped for a chinook. This, we knew, would be our only chance to see these fish alive and up close—actually in hand. Mayer was already in the trap when we arrived, in his waders up to his waist in the Elwha, reaching around his feet to grasp the fish by the tail. After several tries, eventually cornering the fish in the trap, he reached deep then lifted it from the water, silver drops clinging to its massive body. A chinook, for sure.

Thrashing salmon thick as a thigh are not something most people are used to seeing, with jaws long as an ear of corn, snaggly teeth, and big, staring eyes: a live salmon that big was a bit of a shock. A ripe and feisty hen, she squeezed an egg out of her vent; vivid red and glowing, the egg seemed to contain its own light. Mayer worked quickly to measure and weigh the fish and staple a tag in her. With a hole punch, he took a chunk out of her tail for DNA testing. The fish clenched and unclenched her jaws. The first tang of fall was in the air; could she sense it? Morning mist rose from the river, and the sun lit the first yellow leaves of cottonwoods just starting to kite down from the trees. The surface of the Elwha was alive with dancing bugs. Mayer finished up and leaned over the wall of the trap to gently put the fish back in the river, on the other side of the weir, headed upstream. The fish thrashed away, spraying water from her tail as she sped off. We could just see her as a shadow in the river. She looked big as a log.

The weir, among the largest of its type on the West Coast, went in the river for the first time in 2010, and scientists were still testing its value to closely track fish populations before and after dam removal.

That kind of passion for the fish—and for using science to measure and manage the recovery effort—also stoked a simmering dispute. With the dams about to come down, some of the most committed advocates of Elwha dam removal were having second thoughts, because of a new $16 million hatchery built for the tribe as part of the Elwha recovery project. Despite the commemorative sticker distributed by the National Park Service—illustrated with a flowing river, a big leaping salmon, and the motto Elwha River Restoration Natural Wonders Never Cease—this would not be a wholly natural recovery. Instead, fish populations would be pumped up with hatchery fish—maybe even nonnative steelhead, raised and planted by the tribe. Recolonization would also get what policy makers called a jump start, with managers capturing fish returning to the lower river and relocating them to middle and upper reaches of the river and its tributaries.

As the date to take the first whack at the dams approached in September 2011, there was a happy face on the project. The Park Service and locals in Port Angeles, including the tribe, organized festivities, fund-raisers, street dances, speeches, and an invitation-only celebration to commemorate taking the

A weir temporarily erected across the Elwha in late summer is used by scientists to capture, count, mark, and sample adult fish, before releasing them back to the river upstream.

dams down at last. But behind the scenes, amid some of the scientists closest to the project who had backed and promoted dam removal as a victory for nature, it was another story. There was deep disappointment and concern, growing louder and more public, that the hatchery would snatch defeat from the jaws of victory.

Stocking the river from the hatchery would blow a once-in-a-lifetime chance to witness natural recolonization of a river by native species on a grand scale. Left to itself, the river would rebuild fish populations all on its own—there was no doubt of

that. After all, the Toutle River, boiled and turned to mud by the eruption of Mount St. Helens in 1980, was soon alive with steelhead. The eruption devastated most of the anadromous fish habitat in the Toutle River; approximately 90 percent of the upper North Fork and tributaries that had been accessible to salmon were buried by mudflows up to 213 yards deep. Riparian vegetation was stripped from the river's banks. Adult salmon and trout avoided entering the river because of high sediment loads and strayed to other Columbia River tributaries. But natural fish recovery began quickly. The first adult summer steelhead was documented in the North Fork Toutle River in August 1980, just three months after the eruption, and steelhead redds were seen in the North Fork and many South Fork Toutle River tributaries. Incredibly, yearling and older steelhead populations increased tenfold from 1981 to 1984 in a tributary of the South Fork. On the Elwha, even the worst short-term impacts of dam removal would not be as extreme. Every river is different, but the recovery of the Toutle certainly offered some encouragement as to the Elwha's prospects. Recolonization of the Elwha was better than likely; it was expected by scientists whose research showed it was the natural behavior of fish whenever habitat was opened up, from British Columbia's Fraser River to the River Thames in Britain.

But it would take time—in a river as depleted as the Elwha, possibly more time than policy makers were willing to wait for fish to rebuild populations on their own. So instead, adult spawners returning to the lower river would be relocated into the backcountry in trucks, boats, backpacks, and even helicopters, to plant them in wilderness reaches of the river. Hatchery fish would also provide brood stock to bump up populations and provide a genetic safe harbor for Elwha river native runs while the river was choked with sediment. Most controversial was the decision by the tribe to use its new hatchery in part to continue raising and planting nonnative steelhead in the Elwha to provide commercial fishing for its members. The Park Service had built the big new hatchery for the tribe as part of its mitigation program for the Elwha Project because dam removal would render the tribe's old hatchery inoperable.

First planted in the Elwha River by the Washington Department of Fish and Wildlife to thrill sport fishermen, Chambers Creek steelhead now raised by the tribe is a fish

Fish are expected to recolonize the Elwha once the dams are out not only as salmon migrate upstream, but as resident rainbow trout express their genetic ability to go to sea as steelhead in an avalanche of downstream migration.

native to South Puget Sound. The tribe had been stocking Chambers Creek steelhead in the lower Elwha since 1976, to satisfy their treaty right to fish the river as native runs declined. For the sake of the recovery effort, the tribe initiated a fishing moratorium on the river to last five years after the dams had been taken out, but after that, the tribe wanted to fish. And the only fish the tribe believed would be available for harvest that soon after dam removal were Chambers Creek steelhead. So tribal fisheries managers intended to keep right on planting Chambers Creek fish, even after the dams came down, albeit in reduced numbers. However, for some native fish advocates, the hatchery program in the fish recovery plan violated the Elwha restoration act's stated goal of "full restoration of the Elwha River and native anadromous fish therein." They feared the river's native fish, killed off by one hatchery deal a hundred years ago, would be done in again by another.

On the eve of the ceremony commemorating the start of dam removal, the dispute broke into the open. Four wild

In autumn 2010, Kent Mayer of the Washington Department of Fish and Wildlife examines an adult chinook trapped in the weir as a fisheries technician scans it for a coded wire tag. A female, she was then released upriver to spawn.

fish advocacy groups publicly announced the filing of their notice of intent to sue on the basis that the hatchery operations described in the fish recovery plan would violate the federal Endangered Species Act. The suit was formally filed in US District Court in Seattle February 9, 2012, against state, federal, and tribal officials, alleging that for one thing, the Park Service had no business running choppers into a federally protected wilderness to implement not a native fish restoration plan but a commercial fishing enterprise supported by hatchery fish. Some wild fish advocates were so disillusioned they said they'd rather leave the dams in and forget the whole thing. "For my part, the dams are probably better left in, protecting what remains of a wild ecosystem," said Bill McMillan, a retired fish biologist and legendary fly fisherman.

It was entirely predictable. Steelhead—the glamorous gray ghost of Olympic Mountain rivers, the fish of legend and hardest of any species to catch on a fly—creates the deepest divide in Washington State fish politics. Especially online, the disagreement quickly became ugly. It took on the festering overtones of the Northwest's oldest domestic dispute, reduced to caricatures: sport fishermen in noble pursuit of wild salmon on the fly, against tribal fishermen grubbing after disdained meat in the river—hatchery fish—with their despised nets. Both sides had battled over management of Olympic Peninsula rivers for decades. The conflict boiled over again in the high-stakes recovery effort underway on the Elwha.

Underlying all the talk about the hatchery, some of the animus was really the same old chip on the shoulders of sport and commercial fishermen over the Boldt decision—and even flat-out racism. That just made it more difficult for anyone to raise important questions about the hatchery and Chambers Creek fish, for fear of being accused of being against the tribe. Caught in the middle, scientists at every agency that had been invited by the Lower Elwha Klallam Tribe to comment on its Chambers Creek stocking program—from the National Park Service to the Washington Department of Fish and Wildlife, to the National Marine Fisheries Service, to even the tribe's own habitat biologist—nonetheless strongly and clearly advised against the tribe's plan to stock nonnative steelhead in the river. These were not casual communications but official statements on agency letterhead from leading department scientists, backed up with white papers, documented with citations from decades of scientific literature. The critique was unusual in its unanimity: no dueling scientists here.

The scientists found that while Chambers Creek steelhead would provide a fishing opportunity in the river, the fish had no role to play in a restoration plan for native fish stocks, particularly in a national park. Nonnative fish could interbreed with wild native steelhead in the lower river, reducing their fitness. The Chambers Creek steelhead could also stray from the hatchery and, once the dams were out, interbreed with resident rainbow trout in the middle and upper watershed. The likely descendants of the original native Elwha River steelhead, these rainbows were locked up behind the dams like treasures in a jewelbox, waiting now more than a century for a chance to express their urge to go to sea. Hatchery fish could also spread disease and would compete for habitat and food with the native run of wild steelhead. Fishing for hatchery fish could also lead to inadvertent kills of wild fish. It all added up, the scientists wrote, to taking unnecessary risks with a wild native run of steelhead that was down to one hundred to two hundred fish.

Hatchery coho swarm fish food flung in the new, $16 million hatchery built for the Lower Elwha Klallam Tribe as part of the Elwha recovery program. The tribe's initial plan to release non-native Chambers Creek steelhead into the Elwha was controversial.

George Pess had written his doctoral dissertation on fish recolonization and knew deeply the ability of these fish to respond to anything nature threw at them and repopulate the river on their own. "You have to have faith in what works," Pess said. "Ecology happens. Natural systems know how to function. And they do, if you get out of their way." He drew a bright line between politics and science in the decision to stock non-native fish in the Elwha. "If it's about politics, that's fine—say so. But I'll fall on my sword before anyone says it's about science."

However, the Elwha restoration act was not a scientist's document, nor was the Elwha River Fish Restoration Plan,

authored by federal, state, and tribal scientists and published by NOAA's National Marine Fisheries Service in April 2008, a research design for a scientific experiment. Both were mixed bags of practicalities, legal work-arounds, and political necessities. The fish recovery plan sought to balance many goals, some of them competing. Science was only part of the picture. "Were treaty rights not involved and the obligation to provide for continuing fishing opportunities through this transition period not active, then we would not do Chambers Creek," said Will Stelle, Northwest regional director of the National Marine Fisheries Service when I asked him about the controversy not long after the notice of intent to sue was filed. "But those obligations are real, and they are substantial," Stelle said. "Treaty rights are not a bumper sticker. It is a reality, and because of it we have had to reshape and modify the transition program to include a default mechanism to ensure continued modest treaty fishing opportunities, pending rebuilding. And that is where we have ended up. And it is an OK place to be."

He ruled out relying solely on natural recolonization on the Elwha, which, while scientifically feasible, was limited by two practicalities. At the very least, Stelle said, the hatchery was needed as a safe haven for federally protected Elwha River fish as sediment levels in the river spiked when the dams came down. The hatchery was also intended to provide brood stock to speed up repopulation of the depleted river—a policy choice, intended to meet a political goal of seeing some order of restoration within twenty to thirty years. "Waiting fifty or a hundred years for recolonization to rebuild the productivity of the river is too slow," Stelle said, "and losing the genetic legacy we have now doesn't seem to us to be a good idea either. Those are the two primary drivers of continuing an active hatchery program as the bridge between the present and the future."

Some, including Jim Lichatowich, author of the book *Salmon Without Rivers*, saw a fundamental wrongheadedness: Even using the language of "jump-start," he said, betrayed a mechanistic view of what is actually a complex, resilient natural system, capable of recovery all on its own. "The Elwha is not a dead battery," Lichatowich said.

To Jack Stanford, director of the Flathead Lake Biological Station in Montana, the Elwha River and its wild fish weren't getting the respect they deserve. "Dams come out; the salmon respond. Simple as that," Stanford said. He feared a self-fulfilling prophecy: Hatchery fish would depress the performance of wild fish—and create the rationale for keeping the hatchery going. "If you put what I call 'zoo fish' in there to compete with those that would make new habitat their home," Stanford said, "how can that be anything but counterproductive?" He warned too of the record of reluctance to ever close a hatchery—and the challenge of funding the long-term monitoring on which any scientific guidance of the whole enterprise depended. Policy makers put much stock in the promise of so-called adaptive management—namely, a willingness to change course if scientific monitoring showed policies underway were not meeting the goal stated in the Elwha restoration act of recovering self-sustaining runs of native fish in the Elwha.

But, Stelle told me, whether that promise would be kept was a key question that would seal the fate of the Elwha. "Is adaptive management just an empty promise to punt on the hard issues? The answer could be either yes or no, depending on: one, have we structured the system at the outset with the proper types of metrics to discern what success is and measure progress along the way? And [two], are we true to our commitments?" Stelle said.

"It is really a question of political will. Will we have the metrics and the ability to phase out the hatchery if recolonization is working? If we stick to our guns, it will be fine. But if I had one thing to worry about, I would worry about continuing funding to monitor the changes in the river system to track what we are doing and learn. That is by far and away the most important thing. If we fail in that, we will not succeed in the Elwha [restoration] act, and we will not succeed in the promises we have made to ourselves."

■ ■ ■

110 An adult chinook is temporarily trapped in a weir in the Elwha River for scientific data collection. Celebrated for their size and food value, the fish earned the nickname *tyee*—Chinook jargon for chief—among area tribes.

As the dispute flamed away, I toured the new hatchery in August 2011, curious to see it for myself. I'd seen lots of hatcheries, and this one was everything I expected: a gleaming, industrial facility, cement, stainless steel, gravel, and brick, with the best and newest of everything. So new, even the asphalt was clean. It looked, oddly, a little like a power plant.

As we walked around touring the site, Robert Elofson, Mel's brother and river restoration director for the tribe, scooped some pelletized fish food out of a can and winged it into one of the raceways swarming with coho smolts. The surface boiled as the fish chowed down. "Chambers Creek is what we are doing with our funds, at our hatchery," Elofson said. "I don't know why these guys are raising such a big stink about what we are doing."

I asked him about the future—how the tribe would use this hatchery, twice the size of the last one. Could he see ever shutting it down or using it for something other than pumping fish into the Elwha? Maybe, if they started reducing Chambers Creek steelhead, Elofson said, the tribe could raise fish as a business enterprise, stocking hatchery fish in other streams. But that was pure speculation, he noted: "I won't guarantee anything." Job one for him, Elofson said, was a fishable run in the Elwha.

No one had been waiting longer than tribal members, the first to push for dam removal in the Elwha, for a restored fishery in their home river. Nonetheless, in March 2012, as the controversy heated up, the tribe announced that it would provide more time for the discussion and analysis of the problem. The tribe guaranteed in court filings it would hold off on planting Chambers Creek steelhead for one year.

By the fall of 2012, the situation had changed again. The tribe had either destroyed the Chambers Creek steelhead it had been growing at the hatchery or relocated them to lakes with no outlet to the river. It had no more of the fish at the hatchery, nor, at that point, any plan to obtain more. That could always change, Elofson pointed out, but that is where matters stood as the second of the two dams came tumbling down.

Meanwhile, under a plan out for public review, the tribe was poised to catch every adult Chambers Creek steelhead headed back to the river in a fishery at the mouth of the Elwha for the next two winters, to prevent the fish from getting upstream. Talks also were underway to provide a small fishery—just 50 steelhead for ceremonial and subsistence use—after the moratorium expired, if recovery was strong enough. Native Elwha River fish, for the native people of this place.

Once regarded as unthinkable, "Free the Elwha" became a rallying cry for a generation of activists determined to take out the dams. Deconstruction of Glines Canyon Dam continues in this photo in spring, 2012. Both dams would be gone by 2013.

6

DOING THE DEAL

It was, as most people tell it, just another congressional hearing until Bea Charles showed up. As she started to speak in the hearing room of the Senate Energy and Natural Resources Committee in 1992, the usual bored rustling and fidgeting stopped. The committee had heard that day from "a parade of white men," said former US Senator Bill Bradley, recalling the day nineteen years later, in a speech he gave at a dinner in Port Angeles celebrating removal of the dams, which was scheduled to begin the next day. "They're a little harder to remember," he said of the white guys, "but the four women from the Elwha, I remember."

Charles set the tone. Standing at about 5 feet tall, Charles, one of the oldest living members of the Lower Elwha Klallam Tribe, was nonetheless a formidable figure. She still spoke her native language. And, raised along the banks of the Elwha, she still carried the teachings and the memories of the river from her ancestors, as well as her own experience of the river as she was growing up. To her, the river wasn't just a story or a policy debate. It was a way of life she had personally known and experienced. This is what she told the committee:

I grew up on a farm alongside the riverbanks of the Elwha River. I was young at the time that we lived on the farm. But I remember how the fish runs were, because our family used to gather on the bank in front of the house . . . I used to run around, but I saw the fish runs. It was just ripples of salmon going up, and they were big salmon. I remember. I saw it, and I knew that it was there. . . . As the years went by, the fish depleted, and it's to the point where it's nothing. Our Creator gave us this fish to live on, and it was rich and an abundance of fish. It was given to us, and we cherished it and we respected it. We never got more than what we could use. We used it and every bit of it. We didn't waste.

I would like to see the dams removed while I'm still alive. I may not see the abundance of fish come back in my lifetime, but I would like to see it come back for my grandchildren, my great-grandchildren, and the rest of my people, the following generations to come. It was a gift from our Creator. It was our culture and our heritage.

The Elwha restoration act passed later that year. But it would take so long for it to be implemented—nearly twenty years— that Charles, who passed away in her sleep at her home on the reservation in 2009, would not get her wish in this life. Why it took so long—and how a radical idea backed by a motley crew of Indians, tree huggers, and bird-watchers became a mainstream cause for the industrial establishment of Port Angeles—is one of the great stories of the Elwha. "When this was first proposed, it was regarded as not only a pipe dream but a bad idea even within the environmental community," remembered Shawn Cantrell, now executive director of Seattle Audubon but who back then helped lead the charge for the Elwha at Friends of the Earth. "It was, 'It might make sense from a scientific perspective, but you are never going to get it, and it will give us a black eye; this isn't the right campaign battle to take on. It was a pretty extreme issue, wacko; everyone will think we are crazy.'"

For tribal members, the Elwha was always an uphill fight. They did not even have US citizenship or the right to own land until 1924. They had no reservation until 1968—the same year most tribal members finally got indoor plumbing. Even electricity didn't come to everyone in the Elwha valley prior to 1939, despite the power generated by the Elwha dams. But while the dams had provided the tribe no benefits, they were a constant threat. The tribe had been arguing for decades with federal officials for repairs to the Elwha Dam, contending the structure, which had blown out in 1912, was still unsafe. When the license for the Glines Canyon Dam came up for renewal before the Federal Energy Regulatory Commission (FERC)—the Elwha Dam had never been licensed—the tribe saw its chance to finally strike a killing blow. In January 1986, the tribe filed a motion to intervene in the FERC relicensing process, demanding that not only should the dams not be licensed, they should be taken down.

And for the first time in its fight against the dams, the tribe was not alone.

Rick Rutz is an easy guy to underestimate, small in stature, bespectacled, soft-spoken. But Rutz, then on the board and science advisor to Seattle Audubon, in 1984 and 1985 had been poring over maps of the Olympic Peninsula as part of an effort to craft a wilderness designation for Olympic National Park. And he noticed there was a problem with the Glines Canyon Dam. The boundaries of Olympic National Park had been expanded since the dam was built in 1927, and most of its reservoir (Lake Mills) and 2.25 miles of its transmission lines now lay within the park's boundaries. The project, however, had never been grandfathered into the park. And that, Rutz contended, meant that under the Federal Power Act, it could not be relicensed. He saw his opportunity to intervene before FERC, too. "The alliance with the tribe started right there," Rutz said. "That is kind of how it worked. Figure out some things, and then figure out who might be interested."

It was no easy task. "FERC did not like participation by outside parties, so they made a process designed to keep you out; you could make comments, petitions, protests, but none of those counted—they all went in the wastebasket," Rutz said. "The only thing that counted was intervening in the process. Because of my technical training in the sciences, I could produce things to the letter in the way they specified, so I couldn't be excluded for trivial things like formatting." Not a lawyer himself but a seasoned environmental activist, Rutz worked up a motion to intervene in the relicensing process. His handwritten draft on file at the University of Washington Libraries Special Collections, penned on graph paper and pages torn from a yellow legal pad, cross-outs and all, is an

The Elwha has long attracted national attention because of its pristine beauty. Here Robert F. Kennedy and Justice William O. Douglas hike the Elwha valley in 1964. Congress authorized restoration of the Elwha in 1992. (Paul Thomas, *Seattle Times*, 1962)

artifact from the earliest days of the kitchen-table war waged by local Northwest grassroots conservationists against the Elwha dams, long before "Free the Elwha" became the battle cry of a national cause célèbre.

"Several attorneys I talked to said, 'I don't know what to say about it,'" Rutz said of his motion to intervene, based on the dam's presence inside the boundaries of the park. "It looks right to me, but there is no case law on it, so it's hard to give a hard and fast opinion on it. They said, 'We think you have a good case here, and it's worth pursuing it.' There were others who said, 'This is so speculative, you don't even know what you

TIMELINE

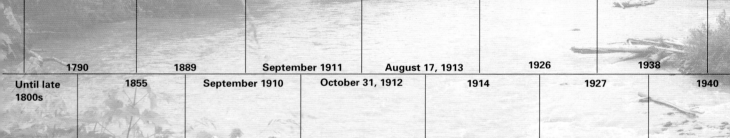

The Klallam are the largest tribe on the Olympic Peninsula of Washington, with villages and camps along the Elwha River, and along both sides of the Strait of Juan de Fuca.

Tribe cedes ownership of land to the US goverment. Lower Elwha Klallam Tribe signs Treaty of Point No Point, ceding ownership of its land.

Construction on Elwha Dam begins. Thomas Aldwell begins construction on Elwha Dam at river mile 4.9. The dam is built without fish passage, in violation of state law.

Elwha Dam blows out, repairs begin.

Electrical generation begins at Elwha Dam.

Glines Canyon Dam becomes operational. No method of fish passage is provided.

Olympic National Park boundary expanded. The park now includes the Glines Canyon hydroelectric site and lands previously held by the US Forest Service.

Crown Zellerbach Corporation files license application for the constructed Elwha Project.

| 1790 | 1889 | September 1911 | August 17, 1913 | 1926 | 1938 | 1968 | 1973 |

| Until late 1800s | 1855 | September 1910 | October 31, 1912 | 1914 | 1927 | 1940 | 1968 |

First European explorer arrives. Spaniard Manuel Quimper is the first documented non-Indian explorer of the Strait of Juan de Fuca.

First organized tour explores Olympics. The Seattle Press Expedition crosses the Olympic Mountains the winter of 1889–90.

Salmon disappear above Elwha Dam. Clallam County game warden alerts state fisheries officials that no salmon appear above Elwha Dam and warns fish run will be destroyed unless action is taken.

Hatchery allowed in lieu of fish passage. State fish commissioner offers to let Aldwell avoid fish passage at the dam, and put in a hatchery instead.

Glines Canyon dam work begins. Construction on Glines Canyon Dam begins at river mile 13.6.

Olympic National Park created. 634,000 acres are designated as Olympic National Park on June 29, 1938.

Indian reservation established. The Lower Elwha Klallam Tribe's reservation is established.

Crown Zellerbach Corporation files applica for relicense Glines Cany Dam.

Sources: National Park Service and The Seattle Times

FERC denied jurisdiction. Department of the Interior asserts that the Federal Energy Regulatory Commission lacks jurisdiction to license Glines Canyon Dam.

President endorses Elwha restoration. President George H.W. Bush signs the Elwha River Ecosystem and Fisheries Restoration Act.

Opposition grows to planned removal of dams. Rescue Elwha Area Lakes (REAL) stirs up opposition to dam removal, decries advocates as a "virgin Earth cult." US Senator Slade Gorton blocks funding for dam removal.

Government purchases both dams. The US Department of Interior purchases both dams for $29.5 million.

Contract awarded for tribal hatchery construction. The National Park Service announces the award of a $16 million contract for a new fish hatchery on the Lower Elwha Klallam reservation.

Lakes behind dams diminish. Lake Aldwell and Lake Mills, the reservoirs behind the dams, are drawn down in preparation for the start of dam removal.

Lawsuit brought against hatchery releases. Wild fish advocates file notice of intent to sue against hatchery releases in the Elwha.

Chinook return. First chinook returns to the river above the former Elwha Dam location.

1986 to 1988   1993   April 1996   August 6, 2004   June 1, 2011   September 15, 2011   March 2012

1979   October 24, 1992   1994   February 2000   September 18, 2009   July 2011   September 16, 2011   August 2012

Tribe and environmentalists petition for dam removal. The Lower Elwha Klallam Tribe intervenes in the relicensing process with the Federal Energy Regulatory Commission and petitions for removal of both dams. Environmental groups—Seattle Audubon Society, Friends of the Earth, Sierra Club, and Olympic Park Associates—join in.

Agency report supports Elwha dams' removal. An Interior Department draft report confirms that both dams need to be removed in order to restore the fish runs.

Elwha Citizens' Advisory Committee in Port Angeles backs staged dam removal.

Dam removal gets final go-ahead. The City of Port Angeles, the National Park Service, and the Lower Elwha Klallam Tribe sign an agreement allowing the $182 million Elwha Restoration Project to go forward.

Power generation is shut down at both dams.

Dam removal begins. Cost balloons to $325 million.

Elwha Dam is history; Glines Canyon Dam is half gone.

Painted by an Earth First activist in 1987, this graffito was just the start of what would become a regional, then national movement to take out the dams. (Tom Thompson, Associated Press)

are talking about.' The National Park Service staff didn't want to hear of it; it sounded way too political, controversial, and crazy. They didn't want anyone rocking the boat. The [government] agencies were asking for piddling concessions, and the [pulp and paper-mill] companies were stiffing them, saying, 'We are getting annual licenses, and as far as we are concerned, we can do this forever.' I said, 'I think you are having major impacts, and I want those dams to come out.'"

Rutz helped convince Seattle Audubon, Friends of the Earth, Olympic Park Associates, and the Sierra Club Cascade Chapter to file the motion for intervention before FERC a few months after the tribe filed its motion, in May 1986. "All the others turned me down because it was too controversial or too crazy," Rutz said. "Here I was talking about tearing out a dam; how irresponsible could you get? And I would say, 'Legally, there is a case for it. And it would do things for the park.' Not only do you not have to be an attorney, you don't have to be a credentialed agency biologist to know a thing or two about this sort of thing, even when they tell you [you] are wrong."

By that time, the dams had only one user: the pulp and paper mill at the base of the Ediz Hook. The dams provided no flood control, no irrigation benefits, and only 40 percent of the power used by the mill. But to the city of Port Angeles, the dams were sacrosanct. So was the mill. Back then, it was the second-largest private employer in Clallam County, with 350 workers, and an estimated direct and indirect impact of $26 million annually in wages and one thousand jobs in the local economy.

The Park Service knew it had a problem with the dams. In a letter from the office of the secretary of the US Department of the Interior—the Park Service's parent agency—to the director of FERC in 1986, deputy associate solicitor David Watts stated only Congress could authorize continued operation of the Glines Canyon project, because FERC had no jurisdiction to license a dam within a national park. Furthermore, the Interior Department's concerns, raised in letters as far back as 1978 and 1980 about the safety of the dams and infringement on beneficial uses of the river, still had not been resolved.

Yet the Interior Department went on record in the same letter as being willing to support relicensing by Congress. In August 1988, William Penn Mott, director of the National Park Service, took a further step back from dam removal, writing FERC to say the Park Service could not support dam removal or even the study of it. "Just commenting or suggesting a study will create much discussion and controversy in the local community," Mott advised. Instead, the agency suggested, why not build a fish ladder over the Elwha Dam and trap and haul adult fish around the Glines Canyon Dam? Why make a fuss and potentially endanger jobs at the mill? "Everyone could win," Mott wrote. "It would be a good example of government agencies working together for the common good and also of a good teamwork relationship between private enterprise and the government."

In its own filings with FERC, Crown Zellerbach Corporation defended the dams as just part of the landscape by now, to which the surrounding ecology of the Elwha had adapted: "The new aquatic biota have long since adjusted to their new habitats and are presently in balance so far as the project and its operations are concerned," Crown Zellerbach Corporation wrote in its application to FERC to relicense the Glines Canyon Dam. "The dam and reservoir have become an integral part of the environment . . . and has very little direct or indirect detrimental effect on the ecology of the land, air, and water environment."

FERC continued to issue annual licenses year after year, pending what seemed an inevitable approval with some sort of conditions. No other agency was asking for much, either: in 1975 the Washington Department of Fisheries traded permanent indemnification for Crown Zellerbach Corporation against all environmental losses on the Elwha in return for the company's contribution of $145,140 toward building a rearing channel to raise hatchery chinook—basically, a concrete slot with netting over it—and paying less than a quarter of its annual operating costs, about $54,000 in 1977. The agency asked nothing for the other species of fish in the river—what was left of them. Wildlife also received no consideration, despite the loss because of the dams of 772 acres of habitat, including 490 acres of migratory big-game range along the Elwha.

But outside the fortress of FERC and the meekness of agencies then in charge, the world was changing. In 1986 Congress passed the Electric Consumers Protection Act, amending the

Federal Power Act for the first time to require FERC to give fish and wildlife protection, mitigation, and enhancement equal consideration with power production and economic need in its consideration of power projects. Even if FERC didn't seem to notice as the Elwha proposal came before it, the tribe and citizen activists did. The Elwha relicensing proposal would be one of the first handled by FERC under the new law. Across the country, relicensing dams was becoming more difficult, technically complex, and expensive for their owners. The Elwha

proposal was unprecedented; it would be the first time FERC would be asked to consider not only a request to not relicense a dam but demands to take it out.

It actually turned out to be FERC that would deliver the first decisive blow for the dam busters, issuing in 1991 a draft environmental impact statement on relicensing of the dams that, under pressure from fish advocates, included an analysis of the cost of taking the dams out compared with the cost of relicensing. It was a breakthrough that advocates for dam

Cheap power from the Elwha dams jump-started the wood products industry in Port Angeles, especially the construction of lumber, pulp, and paper mills that also employed hundreds of men cutting timber in the woods.

removal needed, showing it would be cheaper to take the dams out than to retrofit them for relicensing. "We knew then that we were over the top," Rutz said. "The companies got tremendously scared," he said of James River Corporation, which by then owned the dams, and Daishowa America, which owned the mill. "Their attorneys told them if they kept going before FERC, they would lose, and if they did, they would have no recourse but to declare they couldn't license the dams and they would have to come out. The companies would be standing there all alone; it would be their cost, and if they wanted some way out of it, they'd better settle. We put their back to the wall."

∙ ∙ ∙

Orville Campbell remembers well the visit to his office by staffers from the offices of Democratic US Senators Brock Adams from Washington and Bill Bradley from New Jersey, chairman of the powerful Water and Power Subcommittee of the Senate Energy and Natural Resources Committee. Campbell had worked in pulp mills on and off since 1942, back when the smell of the plant was locally known as the smell of prosperity. He started out working in the paper mill at Port Townsend, baling paper bags three nights a week when he was fifteen years old, for eighty-two and a half cents an hour. "Didn't hurt me a bit," Campbell said, as he shared stories over coffee at a waterfront restaurant in Port Angeles. His straight silver hair was brushed back off a face that had softened with age. So had a lot of his earlier views. Campbell had moved back to Port Angeles in 1973 after working in several other mills. He managed the Elwha dams for twenty-five years—just as environmentalism was beginning to sweep the country. "I came from Louisiana, and I first noticed it down there, in the very

early 1960s," Campbell said. "It was becoming a tremendous influence on industry and commerce. I discovered the hydropower industry had a very bad image. It was evident that the industry as a whole has sort of run roughshod over everyone, and this was beginning to have considerable effect."

Such as, for instance, Congressional staffers sitting in his office that December day in 1991 telling him the party was over. "They said, 'We are going to draft legislation to acquire the Elwha dams and to remove them.' I would have to say it was a bit of a shock, even though I knew there was a lot of talk about removing the projects. They said, 'We are going to shut down the relicensing process, and you have the option of joining us and protecting your industry, or you can ignore it at your peril.' Our entire effort shifted. As a personal goal, I was heavily invested in the process of trying to get the projects relicensed and preserving them for future energy production. Well, it took a few days' reflection to figure out where we were, and of course, corporations are less emotional than people. And so the corporations did join the process of drafting the legislation and incorporating the needs they had, perhaps the most important among them preserving a future supply of energy."

At that time, the Bonneville Power Administration (BPA), the Northwest's supplier of low-cost public power, had been warning industrial customers it might not be able to supply large blocks of energy at its current rates. Suddenly, the mill was looking at the possibility of a sweetheart deal: in return for the James River Corporation abandoning relicensing and giving up the dams, the legislation would guarantee low-cost replacement power by BPA at its current cut-rate price for the Daishowa America mill for forty years. "There were people who thought it was outrageous," Campbell said. "As

It took bipartisan work by a generation of lawmakers in Congress to take down the dams, beginning with US Senator Dan Evans, a Republican. Democratic US Senator Brock Adams, photographed here at Glines Canyon Dam, was a prime sponsor. (Betty Udesen, *Seattle Times*, 1992)

a condition, it was essential. Without energy, the paper mill was not going to run. I had a personal stake in that. At the time there were 350 people working there; it was one of the largest employers in town. They were good-paying jobs; they were the best in town. This was in the 1990s, and [the starting] wage was $15 an hour, with great benefits: full medical [coverage], up to six weeks' vacation. They were very substantial jobs. Even today if the company has an opening, they can get one thousand applicants."

The deal got even sweeter. The James River and Daishowa America companies would bear none of the cost of taking the dams out or restoration to undo their damage. And taxpayers would actually buy the two dams for $30 million. It was a deal unimaginable today—and an offer way too good to refuse. "Getting the government to acquire them was in the companies' interest," Campbell said of the dams. "There was, from the owners' perspective, salvation in all this, given the tremendous expense that would have been incurred in being granted a license. The power costs from those facilities would have been uneconomic. The owners were not in the power business. They were in the paper business. To invest a huge amount of money in those projects would have been wasteful. As it turned out, it was a better deal than if the projects had been licensed."

Uneconomic. The word—its detached calculation—kept ringing in my head as I puzzled it out. Here was a town in love with its dams that for generations had never even gotten along with its own national park. How it had become home to the largest dam removal project ever in the world, run by the Park Service—and why US Senator Slade Gorton led the charge in the US Senate to buy the dams—had never added up for me. Gorton, a former Republican senator for Washington

State, had staked his career, as Washington's attorney general, on working to overturn the Boldt decision, taking his battle through every level of the US court system, before finally losing in the US Supreme Court. By then, Gorton had won the undying opposition of the tribes, which worked hard—alongside environmentalists—for Gorton's defeat in 2000.

But as Campbell told his story, suddenly it all made sense. Of course. Anything but cutting a deal for the companies was uneconomic. So whatever they needed was what was going to happen. For Gorton and the bill's industrial backers in Port Angeles, it wasn't about the river, the fish, the ecosystem, or anything else. It was about a soft landing for the mill in a town in need of a bailout. Fixing the Elwha was green politics all right, but not the kind of green most people thought.

We got up from the table to continue the conversation over at the plant, where Campbell in retirement still kept an office as the mill's official historian, tracking it through its many sales, acquisitions, and reorganizations over the years. Crown Zellerbach Corporation sold its Port Angeles mill and the two Elwha dams to James River Corporation in 1986. In 1988 Daishowa America, a subsidiary of Japanese paper giant Daishowa Paper Manufacturing Company, purchased the Port Angeles mill from James River, but James River maintained its ownership of the dams, eventually changing its name to Fort James Paper Company. It was Fort James that, with Daishowa, eventually negotiated the purchase of the two Elwha dams by the American people for $29.5 million. The US Department of the Interior finally bought the dams in 2000.

As for the mill, it was acquired in a merger with Nippon Paper Industries in 2003 and today is a wholly owned subsidiary of Nippon Paper Group in Japan. But through it all, steam still chuffed from the pulp mill's stack, unspooling into the wind at the base of the Ediz Hook just as it had for more than ninety years. Harold Norlund, resident mill manager, graciously sat down in his office for a talk with me the evening before the dams, which for so long had powered the mill, were due to be unplugged.

I looked around the office. It's not every day you see corporate offices that are shrines to the peninsula's glorious forest products. Wood was everywhere, in heft and craftsmanship from another era. The door to Norlund's office was vertical-grain Douglas fir. Wood cabinets lined the walls. Wood trim. Wood paneling. Norlund sat at a vast desk with a little sliding tray that extended from its front. Presumably, the little wooden tray was for people like me to rest a notebook upon while making notes on the remarks of the big guy—surely it had always been a guy—behind that grand desk. I was game, sliding the lovely tray out for my use. Norlund's in-box was made of wood. Even the caddy for his business cards, on the edge of the desk, was a tiny log, with a slot cut in it to hold his cards.

With the decline of logging on the peninsula, membership in the Association of Western Pulp and Paper Workers union in Washington had steadily declined from a high of more than

To many the Elwha dams had a more than economic value; they were monuments to a work ethic and entrepreneurial ingenuity that transformed the economy of the peninsula. Every rivet in this equipment at Elwha Dam was driven by hand.

22,719 in 1970 to just 5104 in 2010. But the mill still paid good money, $28 an hour on average, straight time, and more—with skilled workers easily making $34 an hour plus full benefits, retirement plans, the works. "This is what US manufacturing was," Norlund said. The payroll at the mill was down to two hundred people—yet the mill was still one of the best things the town had going for it. "We have survived through a lot, and we continue to compete," Norlund said. "We are determined."

The mill had been so powerful for so long, it had never even occurred to people in town anything would ever change. "I remember when I was trying to drum up support for relicensing the projects and meeting virtual disinterest. I would go to public hearings and have a terrible time finding half a dozen people to say, 'We should keep these projects, they are important to our future,'" Campbell said. "When we went to Seattle, we would be outgunned a hundred to one. I spoke to city council members and county commissioners, and none of them were going to get involved. Industry had been here a long time, and everyone assumed it would always be here. They didn't believe it was going to happen. What I saw was, they were taking the industry for granted, that everything would continue the way it was, that there wasn't any real threat. The mills had been here for so long, and they were going to be here forever. I just don't think that people thought in terms of what this was the beginning of. The local Elwha tribe and the national environmental groups were very successful in getting (US Senators) Brock Adams and even Bill Bradley on this, and all this was done way back in Washington, DC, and local folks didn't really know what was going on until pretty much it had happened. Even when the legislation was filed and going through the process, there was strong doubt that Congress would approve it."

The bill's low profile was no accident. Terry Bracy, lobbyist for the mill, worked hard to keep it that way. "We were concerned there would be some tribal and city resentment . . . that some in the city were really going to build a bonfire on this issue. A lot of people in Port Angeles at that time didn't fully understand that this was really a very good deal for Port Angeles and they were likely to get a whole new water system that would allow for growth. But change is hard, and those dams had meaning for the people of Port Angeles." Over

Elwha Dam was never licensed and the license for Glines Canyon Dam expired in 1976. The Glines project also lay partly within the boundaries of Olympic National Park, a violation of federal law seized on by environmentalists determined to block relicensing.

The Federal Energy Regulatory Commission struck the first killing blow for the dam busters, finding in 1991 that it would be cheaper for dam owners to take the dams out than retrofit them to meet modern environmental standards.

about two months, the bill was drafted in Bradley's conference room back in Washington, DC, a feat of shuttle diplomacy for the players from back home.

"The whole strategy was to downplay this as a minor matter. I was very concerned about the interests that could surround this bill: public power, big utilities that didn't want any threat to hydropower," Bracy said. "On the other side, enviro[nmental]

groups would demand more than we could ever get. The louder you got, the more likely it was that you would stir potential opposition. My goal was to shut my mouth. I don't want to say that we were sneaky; we were just very quiet."

It took about six redrafts and several near deaths in committee before the bill was reported out for Congressional action. At that point, it was critical, Bracy felt, to also get the bill passed quickly and quietly—a strategy for which the chaotic closing hours of the legislative session were best suited. "Part of what you have to do when you are trying to slip something through the last day of Congress is, you have to be careful that someone doesn't say something that sets off a fire," Bracy said. "I was up there, and Congress was staying in session for any last few dogs and cats to get through by unanimous consent. It got to be almost one in the morning, and they were about to shut the place down. Finally, the last hours of the last day of the legislative session were ticking by. It was now or never. I was in the members' lobby talking to our allies, Norm [Dicks] and Al [Swift], saying 'Please, just the name of the bill, the title of the bill, and call for a vote.'" Finally in the last minutes of the session, the bill was brought to the floor and passed on a voice vote with no debate. "I think it took less than a minute," Bracy said. Then the news hit back home in Port Angeles.

"When the legislation passed and it sunk in that now these projects are going to be owned by the government, people started to choose sides as to whether or not it was a good idea," Campbell said. "Well, it was a little late." Suddenly the paper plant was in the odd position of fighting for the law, even as the locals rose up to get it overturned.

■ ■ ■

By 1994, the politics of the situation had also turned topsy-turvy. Republican Newt Gingrich had taken control of the US House of Representatives. Gorton, who like every other member of the Washington Congressional delegation had voted for the bill, started to backpedal. It was a pivotal moment. While the Secretary of the Interior that year called for dam removal as the only way to fully restore the river, the Elwha restoration act was not funded. It could still unravel. Rescue Elwha Area Lakes (REAL), a citizens group formed to oppose dam removal, took notice. "They created problems for me and the company, they wanted repeal of the legislation, and they did a lot of lobbying with our legislators," Campbell said.

Meanwhile Norm Dicks, the Democratic member of the House of Representatives who inherited the Elwha in a redistricting, lost Clallam County in the 1994 election. He blamed the Elwha dams. The November 17, 1994, headline in the *Seattle Post-Intelligencer* was "Elwha Dams Plan Is Dead." The paper quoted Dicks as saying, "I think the Elwha dam issue is over. I think that is one we cannot do. The cost is too big. . . . A project like the Elwha, with this GOP majority, is not going to be possible." The story continued, "Dicks, who had been a cautious backer of the dam removal idea until last week's election, said he told [Interior Secretary Bruce] Babbit after the election that tearing down the dams is now a dead issue. 'A big part of this election was to cut spending. I hear the message on it,' Dicks said. 'Welcome to the party,' Gorton said, after learning of Dicks's statement."

Dicks, a former University of Washington linebacker and son of a Bremerton shipyard worker, was seldom intimidated. Packed tightly into his suit jacket, he is the sort of man who always seems like he is shouting, even when he isn't. But he still tells the story of walking into a town-hall meeting in Port Angeles attended by some 150 people: "Someone in the audience jumped up and said, 'Everyone who is opposed to the removal of the dams, stand up,' and there goes three-quarters of the room."

In Port Angeles, REAL kept up a steady drumbeat against dam removal, with leader Marv Chastain warning in the group's newsletter, "Remember, we are up against people on a religious crusade, the Virgin Earth Cult, who will stop at nothing. . . . Their intent is to turn this peninsula into a Virgin Earth park where everything remains forever like they believe it was when Columbus discovered America. No manufacturing or extraction industry, colonized exclusively by the environmental elite who can helicopter in and own nice homes here. Private citizens of the peninsula are under siege."

The Clinton administration by 1993 was already up to its ears in the spotted owl crisis that was shutting down logging in the Northwest's national forests. The last thing it needed was another head-on collision over natural resources in the Northwest. Meanwhile Gorton, holding the Senate's purse strings on funding for dam removal on the Elwha, had found the theme he would ride into battle for reelection in 1994 against a weak Democratic contender, King County Councilman Ron Sims. By then Gorton had honed a political strategy of winning statewide despite widespread opposition to him in the state's most populous city, Seattle, by running hard enough to the right to capture the votes in every rural county of the state.

In floor speeches and on the stump, Gorton started tying the fate of the Elwha to the Columbia and Lower Snake River dams, something advocates of dam removal on the Elwha had

128   The headgate house at Glines Canyon Dam is marooned as Lake Mills drains. Dam removal was nearly defeated after a 1994 political

turnover in Congress, and GOP Senator Slade Gorton, an initial backer of the Elwha act, blocked funding for its implementation.

always been careful not to do. The double-decker headline, all caps, on an eighteen-page press release Gorton put out, read: "ADMINISTRATION ADMITS IT WANTS UNBRIDLED POWER TO REMOVE PACIFIC NORTHWEST DAMS." Gorton had found his issue and a way to stoke some rural backlash.

After the 1994 election, Joe Mentor, a Seattle lawyer in private practice and a former staffer to US Senator Dan Evans, remembered going to a workshop in Port Angeles, scheduled by the Park Service on its environmental impact statement for the project. "I drove into town, and here are these signs: 'Save our Dams. Leave Our Dams Alone,'" Mentor recalled. "I went to the workshop. It was awful. It was, 'You feds leave our dams alone.' I thought, this is major trouble, this is not good. The paternalistic, 'Let us tell you how to solve your problems' had been just terrible," Mentor told me in an interview. "Reasonable people exposed to information will come to the right decision. It's not, 'We live in Port Angeles because we are too stupid to live anywhere else or too stupid to live in Seattle.' The community had real issues. With their back to the water on one side and the federally owned national park on the other, they had nowhere else to go. They felt threatened and pushed around. It had to do with the survivability of their community."

Mentor still felt loyal to Evans, who had long wanted the dams out. A lifelong hiker in the Olympics, Evans had ranged around in the mountains and Elwha valley since he was an Eagle Scout. "Those were great hiking days: none of the fancy equipment, cooking over an open fire, not much in the way of a tent," Evans remembered. "Over time you just get that sense of protection ingrained in you; you cannot spend time in the Olympics without recognizing that every plant, every rock, every stream is important. You learn early on: leave your campsite clean, leave it better than you found it; those things ingrain in you a sense of what is right and what is necessary to protect."

To rescue the Elwha restoration act, Mentor, working with Campbell and Bill Robinson from Trout Unlimited, proposed a strategy of putting together a group of community leaders in Port Angeles not yet associated with the Elwha controversy, to create local backing for dam removal. The Bullitt Foundation in Seattle and other environmental foundations put in the seed money, and the group of eighteen Port Angeles citizens from local business, civic, and government interests started meeting as the Elwha Citizens' Advisory Committee. It was a high-risk strategy, given the backers' lack of control over the outcome.

After months of deliberations on what to do about the situation, in April 1996 the local advisory committee backed federal acquisition of both dams and staged removal, with the lower dam coming out first and the upper dam coming down later, and guaranteed water quality protection. While dam removal would never be embraced by the entire community, with the backing of the local citizens' advisory committee and especially the dams' owners, continuing to stonewall for Gorton made no political sense. It was the rescue the Elwha project needed. In 1997 Gorton put $21 million in the fiscal year 1998 appropriations bill for the US Department of the Interior— enough, with what had already been set aside, to acquire the two dams. He said he still opposed dam removal, but his conservative base felt betrayed.

"Your recent decision to support the removal of the Elwha dams has met with strong opposition among family farmers and ranchers in Eastern Washington. I have talked with numerous people from across the state who are very upset about your decision and are understandably apprehensive about the direction this may lead," Steve Appel, president of the state-wide Washington Farm Bureau wrote Gorton on September 18, 1997. "Despite the promises of security for any other dam over any stated period of time, the removal of the Elwha dams sets a dangerous precedent for the Snake and Columbia rivers. That precedent would have a catastrophic impact throughout the region and the nation. The symbolism of the Elwha dams removal would be just too strong for environmental groups. They just want a dam that they can point to, register it as a victory, and say, 'We did it once, we can do it again.'"

But Gorton, at this point, needed at least to be in line with the recommendations of the mill and the committee speaking for the local interests in Port Angeles. So he pressed on and in 1998 introduced a bill to remove the Elwha Dam and authorize a twelve-year study of the effectiveness of taking it out, before touching the Glines Canyon Dam. The bill also mandated Congressional authorization before any attempt to remove the Columbia and Lower Snake river dams—an unnecessary bone thrown to the dams' advocates since Congress would have to appropriate funds for dam removal anyway. Gorton kept pushing to take out only one dam but narrowly lost reelection the same year.

• • •

Meanwhile, the ground war to actually pay for getting the dams out of the Elwha was just getting started. It would take Dicks, who led the effort, fourteen separate appropriation bills through four administrations and, finally, federal stimulus dollars to pay for the project. "It's the biggest thing I have ever done in my career," Dicks said on the eve of the start of

demolition. Getting buy-in from the locals in Port Angeles was a hands-on proposition, Dicks said. "I personally called every single (city) council member." And it didn't stop there.

Along the way, it still took the promise of dozens of mitigation projects to mollify lingering local opposition and make the Elwha restoration act stick. The eventual $325 million price tag for the Elwha recovery project raised eyebrows—especially the more than $163 million spent on water quality facilities and more than $15 million to operate them, to meet a general promise in the Elwha restoration act to maintain existing water quality for Port Angeles municipal and industrial water users, including the city, the Nippon plant, the tribal hatchery, individual homeowner associations, and well and septic system owners. Building infrastructure for water quality protection swallowed more than half the total eventual spending on the Elwha restoration act, swamped the $113 million original cost estimate for the Elwha restoration, and was by a long shot the single most expensive element of the project. By comparison, dam removal cost $35 million and ecosystem restoration, including revegetation, fish recovery, and scientific monitoring, even less, at $26 million.

Included in the water facilities was a new $30 million water plant for the city of Port Angeles, which already had faced the need to upgrade its municipal water plant, because of tightening state Department of Health regulations. Suddenly, with the Elwha project underway, the city had an opportunity for a twofer.

"This is probably the first and only time the Park Service will build a municipal water-treatment plant," Brian Winter, head of the restoration project for the Park Service, said wearily of the years of negotiations it took to cut a deal with the city over

From this tiny seedling taking root in the former Lake Aldwell, to the grand sweep of the sediment set loose from the mountains, dam removal is unleashing a transformation of the Elwha at the watershed scale.

Implementing the Elwha act cost nearly three times as much as originally projected and most of the spending went not to dam removal, scientific monitoring or restoration but to building water facilities for industrial and residential users in Port Angeles.

its water supply protection. In the end, the city provided the land for the municipal plant. But federal taxpayers paid for construction of the $30 million plant and even kicked in millions of dollars for operating costs. "What we designed goes beyond what probably the Washington Department of Health would have required. There was a long process, then we came along, and the city wanted to use our process to meet their Washington Department of Health needs," Winter said.

Behind escalation in the Elwha project's total cost to nearly triple initial estimates was a combination of factors: inflation in a project that ultimately stretched out over more than twenty years; estimates that were always moving targets;

changed conditions, including the listing of four threatened species in the river; and, most of all, the need to bring specificity to general requirements in negotiations with partners outside the park boundaries that were under no obligation to share costs. "This thing was put together by lobbyists on a golf course. It was a negotiated settlement, with no specifics," Winter said of the Elwha restoration act. "So there you go." But to some, the biggest factor was the city of Port Angeles. "Port Angeles seized on this," said Bracy, the former lobbyist for Daishowa. "Once the bill was passed, they started to dream up a lot of ideas, like the best possible water system in the universe. If they didn't agree, the project wasn't going to happen, and they knew that. The truth of the matter was, I didn't care. I care about the federal budget; I've been in public life for forty years. But to me, this was a magical opportunity. There is no other Elwha that runs out of a national park; it was a unique thing in America, to me, and if you were going to spend another $15 million or $50 million or $100 million, it was worth it. We will find out if we were right. I thought it was worth it, and I did everything I could to sell it. I kept wondering what was taking so long, and the answer was, the city of Port Angeles was dreaming up different projects—and they managed to get them."

Glenn Cutler, public works and utilities director for the city, made no apologies for wringing so much from the taxpayers. At the table representing the city throughout the project, he worked hard to cut the best deal he could. "I have my own opinion about dam removal," he said, driving me to the city's new municipal water plant for a tour. "I do my hunting and fishing at the Safeway." A native of Newark, New Jersey, and a career military man, he answered questions while standing at parade rest as he showed off the gleaming plant, the only one like it in Washington State, with a fancy water filtration system on standby in case the river spat out a particularly dense slug of sediment during the dam removal project. But really, Cutler explained, the filtration enhancement was expected to rarely be used.

I called Gorton the day before the dams were to be unplugged, just to see what, after all these years, he would have to say, especially as he was the one who had repeatedly made cost a centerpiece of his opposition for so long. I was curious to see if time perhaps had mellowed him. "I don't see any reason to be interviewed on this subject; I see no reason to cry over spilled milk," he said when I reached him at his Seattle law office at the international firm of K&L Gates. "It was Norm's deal; he should know how it was accomplished," he continued, "For better or worse, this is all Norm (Dicks.) It's water long over the dam," he said, in no way making a pun. "It is something with which I disagreed, and I just don't want to be reminded of it."

I asked him why. "The first thing is the money," he said. When I told him what the project actually wound up costing, he sounded genuinely surprised. "Oh, my gosh. Really. I thought it would be a lot less than that, a whole digit less than that. There are still people out there who don't like it and think it's too much. I always separated the upper and the lower dam."

Yes. Another one of the reasons the project took so long and cost so much. But the former senator did not wish to discuss it. "This is not going to be something I celebrate. And it is something in the past," Gorton said. And with that, he hung up.

Jim Adelman of the Smithsonian Migratory Bird Center untangles a mist net
to string across the river to temporarily capture dippers, an aquatic songbird,
for his work studying the effects of dam removal on birds.

7

BARNUM'S MENAGERIE

Jim Adelman stood in a tributary of the middle Elwha, patiently plucking at a mist net like a harpist, trying to dislodge leaves and twigs stuck in its fine web. Intended to catch songbirds, at the moment the mist net was capturing leaf litter with admirable tenacity. Twig tangle, leaf tangle, net tangle. These were not laboratory conditions.

"So glad you are filming this," said Adelman, a postdoctoral researcher from the Smithsonian Migratory Bird Center, with good-natured sarcasm as Steve brought his video camera in for the close-up. It was early spring 2011, and Adelman was looking for the salmon in the songbirds. By clipping off bits of their toenails, snagging a tail feather, and getting a sample of blood in a vial, all to be analyzed back at the lab, he wanted to learn if the birds carried a signature of nutrients derived from the marine environment in their bodies. Birds eating salmon eggs—or larvae that had preyed on salmon carcasses or bugs that had eaten those larvae—should show traces of nutrients from the fish in their blood and tissues, Adelman knew. So by sampling the birds, he could learn how deeply into the watershed the nutrients from the fish traveled, through the vectors of the birds. He was sampling dippers, because of their dependence on the river for food. Other songbirds interested him too, in the uplands along the river. He wanted to know how far from the river the influence of the salmon reached.

But first he had to get the mist net untangled. It hung in a knotted heap, limp in his hands. "Must have put this away quickly," he said, finally unknotting the mess and pounding in stakes to stretch the mist net across the river. "What we are trying to do now is get a baseline," Adelman said. "So that you can see ten, twenty years from now, after the dams have come out, if that marine-derived signature comes back into the birds, into the things that are feeding on whatever is in the river." Later, at an inland site, Adelman dug his all-purpose fix-it tool from his pocket to fit two sections of pole together so he could string his net for another try.

I settled into the slumped-over tussocks of uncut grass to watch and wait as he slung the mist net in a meadow on the tribe's reservation, by the lower river. The net was so fine as to be nearly invisible. The call of a song sparrow told us we might soon be in luck. Within moments the bird cruised into the net, and Adelman was on his feet, running to untangle it from the mesh. He put the bird in a small white cotton bag and hung it from a branch as he worked to set up his sampling kit. The bird fluttered, the bag swaying with its efforts, as Adelman prepared to get to work. "There you go, buddy," he said softly, sliding the bird from the bag and getting it in position, holding its head loosely between two fingers as he surveyed its plump, warm body. He blew on its feathers to part them, checking to see if the bird was in breeding condition, and quickly got a blood sample. The bird looked back at him, blinking but not struggling. Within moments Adelman was finished and opened his hand, releasing the bird in a whirring flutter.

Carcasses of spawned-out salmon feed a wide variety of wildlife—at least twenty-two species, researchers studying Olympic rivers have learned. Bald and golden eagles, northern goshawks, Pacific fishers, peregrine falcons, pileated woodpeckers, Vaux's swifts. Bears, raccoons, ravens, gulls. Mink, pine martens, and long-tailed weasels. Belted kingfishers and common mergansers. Coyotes and river otters. Even squirrels, deer, and garter snakes—the Barnum's menagerie Private Harry Fisher noted on his sleepless night by Queets in the nineteenth century, when he was kept awake by the thrashing salmon and feasting animals.

The lives of land animals and birds and the lives of fish, though often treated as separate ecological communities, are clearly linked through the food chain, with salmon and steelhead acting as the silvery shuttle that interweaves their aquatic and terrestrial realms. Two nutrients, phosphorus

A blood sample from this song sparrow will help Jim Adelman learn if it carries a signature of nutrients derived from fish, and how far from the river the influence of salmon in birds' diets can be detected.

and nitrogen, often limit biological productivity in Northwest rivers. But each year, under natural conditions, decomposition of salmon carcasses in the Elwha probably provided more than 13,000 pounds of these nutrients to the river. The nutrients were absorbed by aquatic plants and animals, forming the base of an in-stream food chain that fed, among others, juvenile salmon and trout. Even distant from the river, the land benefits from the salmon's gift of food from the sea, as animals such as bears bring fish carcasses to their deep forest lairs and defecate the nutrients from their salmon meals, feeding the

Dippers, or water ouzels, are native to the Elwha. Soon after the first salmon and steelhead spawned above what used to be Elwha Dam, biologist John McMillan witnessed dippers dining on their eggs, a tiny reboot of the Elwha's food web.

soil. C. Jeff Cederholm, lead author on a 1988 paper published in the *Canadian Journal of Fisheries and Aquatic Sciences*, documented the fate of 945 coho carcasses his team planted on seven spawning streams on the Olympic Peninsula. They recorded forty-three species of mammals and birds present and found that 51 percent of them fed on coho carcasses, from black bears to tiny shrews. It started, typically, with raccoons, river otters, and bears retrieving carcasses from streams, with bears pulling fish from pools more than 5 feet deep, feeding, and then moving on. Over the next several weeks, the scattered remains were fed on by small mammals and birds, until

only a few bones remained, with tiny tooth marks on the bones and skinned fin rays and lower jaws showing the urgent work of the clean-up. Dippers, jays, eagles, crows, and ravens joined in, too. Even salmon, the researchers learned, ate salmon. Juveniles fed on salmon carcass flesh, salmon eggs, and aquatic bugs that previously fed on salmon carcasses: caddis flies, stone flies, midges, and stone-fly nymphs. Other animals depended on those bugs too, including salamanders and frogs, both as swimming juveniles and, later, as land-based adults.

Research by Sarah Morley, Jeff Duda, and their colleagues at fifty-two research spots in the Elwha from 2004 to 2006 also found that in the lower river, where salmon still had access, nitrogen isotope ratio levels were higher in fish, stone flies, blackflies, and algae than in other areas of the river where dams blocked salmon migration. These stable isotope ratios are used in ecology as tracers of an animal's diet. The tissues of salmon have an isotope signature that reflects their time feeding in the ocean, which in turn can be detected in freshwater organisms that feed on salmon carcasses and eggs in the Elwha. The standing crop of periphyton was higher below the dams too, and the population of bugs was different in research sites above the dams from sites below them.

To further test the linkage between salmon and nutrient cycling in the environment, Morley and other members of the monitoring team from 2006 to 2008 had placed salmon carcasses in side channels of the river and found that afterward both periphyton growth rates and nitrogen isotope levels in the bodies of juvenile salmon were elevated. The difference was big enough to suggest the powerful role returning salmon might one day play in this river. Nitrogen isotope levels were still significantly elevated as many as three months after fish

Predators such as eagles, rarely seen in the middle or upper reaches of the river before dam removal, are expected to return to the Elwha watershed to feast on the gift of salmon and steelhead.

Elwha dam removal is more than a fish story. It is an ecosystem-wide restoration, affecting the entire watershed, including 800 acres of home range habitat inundated by dam floodwaters that have been returned to elk and other wildlife.

carcass placement and detectable in many levels of the food web, from the slime on the bottom to algae-grazing mayflies to juvenile fish. Some of the biggest increases were seen at the very base of the food chain, with periphyton nitrogen isotope levels twice as high where the carcasses had been placed and growth rates three times that of other reaches some 600 feet upstream that lacked carcasses. Juvenile steelhead showed nitrogen isotope levels 30 percent higher than nearby reference reaches without salmon carcasses.

To fill out the picture, the team would add the data gathered in 2010 and 2011 from the drift net and fish diet sampling we had witnessed, to track short- and long-term food web responses to taking the dams out. If just a few salmon carcasses placed by researchers created a measurable nutrient bump, what if pink salmon, which used to throng this river a quarter million strong but today are depleted to nearly nothing, came back?

But salmon are even more than food: they are also change agents, affecting the range and distribution of animals that feed on them, and in some instances, even affecting the breeding biology of those animals. In the Elwha, the range and movement of a wide variety of animals throughout the watershed is expected to change as they respond to regular, predictable supplies of food with the salmon's migration restored to the middle and upper reaches of the river. From the tiniest creatures at the base of the food chain in the bottom of the river to the Elwha's biggest and most charismatic animals—Roosevelt elk and black bears—dam removal is predicted to make a difference.

. . .

To understand how animals were using the watershed prior to dam removal, the Lower Elwha Klallam Tribe hired Fox Sam and Rebecca Paradis to track and tag Roosevelt elk in the tribe's traditional hunting area. The elks' range patterns were expected to change once the river was back in its natural channel, formerly important winter range for elk. But learning anything about them and their movements first meant finding them.

On a drizzly spring morning in 2011, we went along for a tracking expedition, meeting up with Sam and Paradis at a park-and-ride lot along US 101 outside of Port Angeles. The researchers weren't hard to spot: geared up in full camouflage, with rifles at their sides, these had to be the people we were looking for. We exchanged hellos as they opened the back of their rig and reached for a proven lights-out tranquilizer, drawing up a dose into darts long as their hand. With a few pumps, the carbon dioxide chargers on their rifles were ready to fire, in case Fox and Paradis got lucky with the elk. I hopped in the back to ride with them as Steve drove along behind with all his camera gear.

We headed down the highway to the back roads that would take us to the unpaved logging roads threading so much of the landscape outside the park, into forests that climb ridge after ridge above the Elwha. Paradis took the wheel; Sam, twenty, pounded Doritos and glugged fruit punch from a gallon plastic jug. A member of the Upper Skagit Tribe, Sam had grown up hunting elk in these woods. Paradis, a non-Indian single mother of four, was a relative newcomer to field biology. They seemed an unlikely duo at first. But they had worked up a camaraderie in their days in the woods, tracking elk together. There might be one elk in 300 acres. In six months, they'd had only two clear shots at their quarry and managed to get a radio collar on only one animal.

They went out in any weather, starting their day at 6:30 AM to catch the elk at first light, when they might be on the move. The goal was to eventually fit twenty elk with radio collars that transmit a signal to a satellite. The data would be sent in email dumps to the tribe's wildlife biologist four times a day, documenting the elks' location, so the animals' distribution and seasonal movement could be plotted on a map.

Paradis was a late convert to the career of a wildlife field technician, working her way into her job through sheer interest and persistence, first as a volunteer. "I feel like I get a chance to leave something better than I found it," Paradis said. "And I love being outside." Good thing. As we bailed out of the vehicles, a soft rain fell and mist twined in the tops of the trees. They knew their drill without needing to talk about it, moving silently into the brush with their dart guns. "They are prey animals. They can smell, hear, and see you," Fox said of the elk in these hills. "You get that adrenaline rush, being that close to a big animal." Very close, hopefully. For, unlike bullets, the darts would deflect if they hit brush. "We need an open 30-yard shot," Fox said and melted into the salal.

A Pacific chorus frog kreeeecked in the woods; pine siskins chattered in the hemlock and fir. We walked the logging road,

THE ELWHA RIVER: VISION OF A RESTORED ECOSYSTEM

When the dams were constructed, they disabled what was once a chaotic, noisy, life-filled river. The salmon could no longer swim upriver to spawn. Trees were no longer nourished by the nitrogen-rich remains of salmon dragged into the woods by predators and scavengers. Eagles and river otters dwindled in the upper reaches. Restoring the river and watershed is a complicated process that could take as long as one hundred years.

POPULATIONS
Salmon are expected to vigorously recolonize the river once habitat is available. On land, animals are expected to come back to take advantage of returning salmon. Native plants will be restored, and weeds controlled in bare areas when reservoirs drain.

PROCESSES
Dam removal will restore the river to its role as conveyor belt, transporting large woody debris, sediment, cobbles, and gravel from the mountains to the sea.

SHAPE
Unimpeded by the dams, the Elwha will be more able to meander back and forth across the floodplain, cut side channels, build logjams, pools, and gravel bars, and deposit gravel spawning beds and sandy beaches.

POPULATIONS: Plants
Native species will naturally recolonize or be replanted, including cottonwood, red alder, and Douglas fir. Woody plants such as snowberry can spread fast and help stabilize new ground. Invaders, including knotweed, Himalayan blackberry, reed canary grass, and herb Robert, will be controlled.

POPULATIONS: Fish
Salmon are a food source for wildlife in the Elwha watershed, from eagles and osprey to black bears and river otters. Fish bring marine-derived nutrients back to the watershed, connecting the land, the river, and the sea. It's hoped the river will once again be home to robust runs of all five species of salmon.

PROCESSES: Sediment
Dam removal will release sediment, cobbles, sand and other substrates trapped behind the dams. Salmon need gravel to build their nests, and beaches have been starved for sand.

SHAPE: Multiple channels
Scientists have mapped more than 26 miles of side channels in the floodplain of the Elwha, and the river is expected to make more when the dams come down. They are fed both by ground and surface water, adding to the river's diversity of habitat.

PROCESSES: Speed, temperature
Dams slow river currents, allowing water to heat and reach sometimes lethal temperatures for cold-water fish like salmon. The natural, free-flowing river will run fast and cold.

Carcasses and feces left on the forest floor by salmon predators and scavengers feed plants, bugs and other animals.

Roosevelt elk

Bald eagle

River otter

PROCESSES: Woody debris
Natural rivers move around an chew their banks, felling trees that jam in the channel and cre gravel bars, pools, and side channels. The logjams built by river create islands of stability where a new forest can grow.

Black bear

SHAPE: Side channels
Side channels give salmon refuge from the cold, fast-moving waters of the main channel. Side channels are expected to be an important refuge for salmon during the first ten years of dam removal, when the river is flushing out heavy sediment loads trapped behind the dams.

Biologists radio-collared thirteen bears and learned that without salmon, bears stay in the high country, eating berries.

Side channels give young salmon a chance to grow bigger, boosting their chances of survival.

Salmon

Biologists are tracking river otters to see if their behavior changes when salmon return to the river.

Note: Not to scale

A. RAYMOND/THE SEATTLE TIME

Source: National Park Service

then picked our way through salal and underbrush. By morning's end, we saw no sign of the elk but a goodly pile of elk pellets—yet even that had its use for Sam and Paradis: to estimate the population of animals using the area. "What keeps me going is, there's something about stalking up on something that hard," Sam said. "Rifle hunting is easy."

Skunked but still wanting to see and photograph one of the collared elk, we headed back to the reservation to meet up with Kim Sager-Fradkin. She shared her office with heaps of waders, boots, and piles of coats, the necessaries of a field biologist. The first wildlife biologist ever hired by the tribe, she dialed in the latest data from the only elk collared in the project so far. "She just emailed me," Sager-Fradkin said of the cow, scrolling through the data. Grabbing the radio antenna, we headed out to pick up her signal.

I expected the cow to be in some noble redoubt deep in the bosom of the Elwha watershed. Instead, she was reposing in a pasture off a back road not a half hour from downtown Port Angeles, just passing the drizzly day with a herd of her buddies. Chewing, snoozing, stretching, she finally stood, shaking the rain from her lush coat like a dog, the big yellow collar looking like a fur stole on a doyenne at the opera. The collar would transmit for five years and should provide a rich trove of data on the movement of this herd, the largest in the Elwha, Sager-Fradkin said.

How the animals' use of this area would continue to change as the reservoirs drained, returning valuable lowland winter range, was just one of the questions she was working on. She'd spent the previous summer in the upper reaches of the Elwha collaring black bears to determine if their movements also would change once they had not only berries to eat in the high country but salmon in the river. She was also collaborating with Adelman on his research. Working together, they hoped to put together a picture of how watershed restoration affected river-dependent species of birds and mammals. Adelman already had the bird end covered, with his work on the dippers. To bring in the mammalian side of the picture, Sager-Fradkin was live-trapping river otters, which, like the dippers, depend on the river for their food supply.

Sager-Fradkin decided to set traps in the lower, middle, and upper river to capture the otters, then transport them to a veterinarian on standby to implant a radio transmitter under the animals' skin. Blood, tissue, and scat samples would reveal the presence of marine-derived nutrients in their bodies as well, and with the transmitters in place, she'd be able to track their seasonal movements once released before and after the dams came down. That was the idea anyway. But first, like Adelman, Sam, and Paradis, she had to catch her subject.

"I am not happy with this trap at all," Sager-Fradkin said back in the office, as she screened photos from a tree-mounted camera that showed otters feasting on fish she had left in one of the traps. The otters were captured on film enjoying their meal, then scampering right on out of the trap, the door never even closing on their way out. A cougar slinked past in the background in one of the grainy black-and-white images. In the morning, we planned to check the traps in the lower river to see what was going on.

It rained hard all night, a real rain-gutter-rattling soaking that the Olympics deliver so very well. I wondered what riverside fieldwork was going to be like in the morning. But the day broke gray and calm without a bit of wind, the rain wrung out from the clouds that stretched in an undifferentiated ceiling to the horizon line. We met at Sager-Fradkin's office and she introduced us to the field techs we'd be working with: a nineteen-year-old from the Lower Elwha Klallam Tribe and a seventeen-year-old non-Indian student intern. Sager-Fradkin stayed behind, and we headed out the back door of the fisheries building, walking to the site by the lower river.

Dogs ranging around out by the old hatchery ponds came tail-wagging over as we crossed the potholed and puddled gravel parking lot. The two teens took out after the dogs in a game of chase, free and playful. We crossed the levee and arrived at the end of the road by the river. The tide was up, pushing into the river, forcing the water up the banks. The riverside path was underwater at high tide, so we made our way through the thickets of underbrush along the shore. I pushed into thimbleberry and salmonberry tangles that clawed my hat off and heaved myself over moss-jacketed downed logs. The soft ground sucked the sole of one of my old muck boots right off its tacks while the kids barreled ahead as if over flat, clear ground.

The Indian plum was just breaking bud in the early spring, its fresh green leaves upright like praying hands. Its tresses of delicate white blossoms were the first flowers of the year. Something stank. Of course—the bait. Arriving at the first trap, one of the kids knelt down and barehanded the drippy, rotting head of a steelhead, lobbing it into the river where it abruptly sank. Seals bobbed just downstream, their heads doming the water's surface. Eagles chittered in the trees; mergansers floated serenely in the slate-green waters of the lower river, simplified and jacketed in levees today to one channel. Years ago, old photographs show it was three. We were so low in its reach we could see the broad estuary where the Elwha finally slid into salt water.

The two worked smoothly as a team, each knowing his and her job and setting about it with zeal. They were supporting each other in the work of checking the motion-triggered camera in the tree, changing the bait, and messing with the trap's door, trying to get it to close more readily to improve their capture success. I was struck by how well they worked together.

The river for years now had been the center of an ongoing investment by the tribe in the youth of its community, Indian or not. Kids of all races were learning about Klallam history and culture, often for the first time, in an Elwha curriculum created by the tribe and taught in the Port Angeles public schools. Outside the classroom, the Elwha Science Education Project paired tribal elders and instructors with professional geoscience educators in the field in the tribe's former lands at Olympic National Park, to blend cultural instruction with scientific curriculum, culminating with a presentation by the students to the community.

"The first year we did it, ten parents showed up. Last year, seventy-five people came, not including the kids," LaTrisha Suggs, who helps coordinate the program for the tribe, told me in November 2011. "We want to spread it out in the other sciences involved in the restoration, so we can widen the focus of the program." Robert Elofson, the head of river restoration for the tribe, said, "We have six or seven jobs in natural resources, and we want our tribal members to start filling these positions. LaTrisha and I both have our college educations; we had a large graduation group last year, the largest that Elwha has ever had. The tribe takes a great deal of pride that we have been involved in this [restoration project] from the start, and we are a major reason why this is happening."

Researchers carry a river otter trapped along the Elwha. They are studying the travels and diet of animals such as otters that depend solely on the aquatic environment to learn how or if their movement and diet change after dam removal.

Just as the project was rejuvenating the tribe, so too was it already sparking new life in the watershed. In the spring of 2012, there were signs everywhere of animals utilizing the habitat returned to them.

The muddy gray banks along the river, where Elwha Dam once stood, were crisscrossed with the hoofprints of deer and the tiny tracks of racoons and beavers. Pools of freshwater ponded along the shore were alive with caddis-fly larvae. The soft, wet mud around the pools was crosshatched with the tracks of killdeer feasting on the bugs. Fish biologists working in the area saw the tracks of bears and mink and watched water ouzels eating salmon eggs. Carcasses of the coho salmon they

had released to spawn above the dams during the winter had disappeared—a long-awaited feast nourishing the animals of the watershed. Construction workers clawing out the lower dam in March also had seen a river otter with a fish in its mouth, successfully hunting even in the sediment-choked waters.

It was fish biologist John McMillan who saw the first known wild adult male steelhead return to the Elwha, in May 2012. He saw the 35-inch-long fish in the Little River, a tributary of the Elwha, seeking out females with which to spawn. It was the first known wild fish crossing what had been the lower dam site in a century, where the river now ran free.

Kim Sager-Fradkin, wildlife biologist for the Lower Elwha Klallam Tribe, checks a trap for river otters to make it close more quickly. It's baited with a hunk of steelhead.

McMillan and Lower Elwha Klallam tribal fisheries worker Raymond Moses also saw spawning redds in Indian Creek, more evidence that fish were already making it past the former dam site, in a place where researchers had not relocated steelhead to jump-start recolonization. The fish were moving back home all on their own. Less than five months after taking down Elwha Dam, the first chinook also were seen back in Olympic National Park, a triumphant return of the kings to their ancestral spawning ground.

Dam removal was only half completed. But fish and wildlife, from tiny caddis flies to mink, bears, and wild native steelhead, were already coming back, reclaiming their place in the great house of *tyee*.

In 2011, Lower Elwha Klallam tribal member Rachael Hagaman, right, and her sister Lola Moses weave a cedar bough raft to ceremonially return to the Elwha chinook caught below Elwha Dam. The tribe's next catch would finally be from a free-flowing river.

8

THE POWER OF PERSISTENCE

Fog was ghosting over the Elwha so thick I couldn't see the opposite shore. Rachael Hagaman and her sister Lola Moses were weaving a raft of cedar boughs by hand, working at a folding table they'd brought down to the banks of the lower river on the tribe's reservation. The raft was for the guests of honor: just five chinook salmon, the last the tribe would catch in the Elwha before the dams came down.

Caught by Sonny Sampson and Mel Elofson, the fish had already been cut so pieces of the meat could be gifted to the tribe's elders. Honored today would be the remains of the fish, carefully preserved with their heads, tails, and skeletons intact. They would be returned to the river in a First Salmon ceremony traditionally performed in the village to ensure the salmon's return.

It was Hagaman along with Shaker Church minister Bosco Charles, who, in about 1990, helped bring the First Salmon ceremony—not performed in the Lower Elwha tribal community for many years—back to the Lower Elwha people. "I was fish manager at the time," Hagaman told me on the phone, before Steve and I traveled over for the ceremony in August 2011. I asked her how the effort to bring the ceremony back to the community got started. It was, it turned out, all of a piece with the tribe's work to take out the dams. "We had a big, long battle ahead of us in terms of removal of the dams," Hagaman said. "I felt blessed to be . . . part of the solution at the time. It's been a blessing, a long time coming. Our ancestors cried a lot when the dams went in. Their voices were not heard. I think about the ancestors who originally had the fight; they tried, but they were not allowed to be heard. The elders said every river has its people. Wherever there was a river delta with a major watershed, that is what sustained them." Now the tribe's director of economic development, Hagaman also fished the sockeye season hard.

The raft was nearly finished, readied to carry the remains of the tribe's first salmon catch to the Salmon People, dwelling in houses under the sea. In Coast Salish teachings, honoring the first salmon of the year by returning their remains to the river would encourage the salmon to return, ensuring

a bountiful harvest. Hagaman had also been taught by her grandmother, Laverne Ulmer Hepfer, that the ceremony traditionally brought the tribe's fishing and hunting villages—located farther upriver—together to celebrate, share, and give thanks.

The tribe's push for dam removal began well before her generation, Hagaman said. "I remember her saying, 'We need to take those dams out,'" she said of her grandmother. "'How are we going to do that?'" Not whether, notice, but how.

The women worked bare-handed in short-sleeved summer tops, not heeding either the chill fog that had me wrapped in a wool scarf or the bloody carcasses of the fish. There was a peacefulness to their work and also a joyfulness, as kids from the reservation day care arrived, pulled in a wagon by their teacher. Two dogs swirled about, playing. Members of the tribe's fisheries and hatchery department started to arrive, including the non-Indians, seeking perhaps a connection to the spiritual underpinning of their work.

A rumble down the road turned every head to see Phil Charles, a former tribal council member and Vietnam veteran, arriving on his Harley, souped-up with aftermarket pipes. Dressed in black leather chaps, his gray ponytail swishing as he dismounted, he exchanged hugs with his relatives. Mark "Hammer" Charles—named for his trademark style on the basketball court in high school—had brought his hand drum and his four-year-old grand-nephew, Roger Tinoco-Wheeler. Baby Roger to my husband and me—we had known him since his birth. Seeing Hammer and Baby Roger here brought home the gift of the renewal of this ceremony, carrying the tribe's culture to yet another generation. I asked Hammer how he felt about the dams starting to come down in just about a month. He

To tribal members such as Mark "Hammer" Charles, left, salmon are at the heart of a way of life.

raised his forearm to show me his tattoo: a fishhook. Hammer remembered when he could snag twenty fish in the river in two hours. "You train your eyes enough, that's what happens; you know where the fish are sitting. I come from a fishing family. And I have fished this river for a lot of years," Charles said. "All these things I am doing, I am doing for him," he said, looking at Baby Roger. "I just live life. I get to sit here and sing with my four-year-old grand-nephew—that is something I will do the rest of our lives, carrying on these traditions."

Pat John, an Ahousaht First Nation member from Canada living at Lower Elwha, had tied his waist-length braid back with a traditional Cowichan wool headband. He and Hammer took up their drums and offered a song, the music twining with the fog as Hagaman and Moses put the finishing touches on the cedar-bough raft. Hammer had been teaching Baby

Roger traditional Klallam songs since he was born. In a culture in which songs are a family's wealth, his family was rich, with twenty family songs alone. Baby Roger, standing no higher than Charles's knee, belted out an arrival song for the fish, his voice much bigger than seemed possible. They kept it up until Ben Charles Sr., a Lower Elwha Klallam elder and Shaker minister, was ready to offer the blessing. He wore traditional regalia made for him by his niece Jamie Valadez: a black vest with a red thunderbird on each side of the front. In the tribe's teachings, Thunderbird could chase salmon up the Elwha to feed the people just by beating its wings and flashing its eyes.

The river whispered past. There wasn't a puff of wind. Even the dogs had quieted. Ben Charles offered a prayer. "I'm glad for all the reviving, the first salmon," Charles said. "Our community welcomes the first salmon back and sends the spirit

When Elwha Dam was built its floodwaters inundated the tribe's sacred creation site upstream, as well as its largest inland village site, and lands up and down both banks of the river used by tribal members for centuries.

of the first salmon catch where it needs to go. Tell them: 'These people love us, they need us, this is where we need to go. C'mon.' Then all kinds of salmon will come up this river." When the dams went in, Ben Charles said, it created confusion for the Salmon People. "But now when the dams come down, they will once more go up and be home. That is the great thing that is happening in our village. And I am thankful, for all the ones in our community, that all the things that have been a hurt for so many years will heal over. Our prayers are answered. It might take years. Some of us lose patience with all that is happening. There's many times we are going to pray that the spirit of the salmon will again be strong, coming on the great ocean, along the Strait and the river. May they be plenteous and strong. Be with us in the next month as we dismantle the dams. Give the salmon a passageway, up to their homes."

With the prayer finished, Hammer and John and Baby Roger began once more to sing, as Hagaman and her sister placed some of the carcasses of the fish on the cedar raft for Charles to help carry to the river's edge. She saved the rest to release in two other locations on the river: in the middle, between the two dams at the Altair Campground in the national park, and above the Glines Canyon Dam, in Lake Mills. The fishes' tails bore the trademark spots of chinook, the most prized fish of all. Hammer and another tribal member gently pushed the raft into the water for the river to carry downstream, back to the home of the Salmon People. The water flowed right through the cedar boughs, over the faces of the fish.

As the green raft with its crimson and silver burden floated on the current, everyone gathered on the banks to watch as the last big kings to be taken from this dammed river were returned to it, carrying with them their prayers for a river reborn.

Hagaman piled into a pickup with the remaining fish to release them upriver. I walked over to her to say good-bye. "It's such a blessing to see this start happening and know it's going to become real," she said, tears in her eyes. "All kinds of people, all kinds of agencies worked on it; it's going to happen. I'm just so grateful it's going to come in our lifetime; it's an answer to our ancestors' prayers. They were always thankful because the river provided enough for them."

I walked from the river down to the tribal center and found Frances Charles, chairwoman of the Lower Elwha Klallam Tribe and a direct and powerful woman. I had first met her on a reporting trip in 2004, after construction contractors

Tribal members paid the heaviest price for the Elwha dams, yet saw little of their benefits. For them, jobs remained scarce, and electricity was not widely available in their community until 1968— provided not by the dams, but by the Bonneville grid.

inadvertently unearthed Tse-whit-zen, the tribe's largest known village site and burial ground. Now here was the tribe at another defining threshold. "It's going to be history, not only for the Elwha Klallam tribal people, but nationally," she said. "We were always told it would never happen. It is going to be an overwhelming day. I think about all the work, the effort, over all the generations. It's a process of restoring what was lost.

"It's about our ancestors and those before them; we are walking in their footpaths, all the ones before us. They are the

Adeline Smith, ninety-three, one of the oldest members of the Lower Elwha Klallam Tribe, said she had seen a lot of changes in her life. But the dams coming out? She said, "I never thought I would see the day."

ones we want to recognize and whose footsteps we are following. These were the foods our people lived off. The fish [that] people were beaten and arrested for, to provide food for the table. How do I feel? I don't even know; we have been talking and dreaming about this for so long."

. . .

At Lower Elwha, almost no living person had been talking and dreaming about taking the dams down longer than Adeline Smith. I had gone to see her that spring, one of many visits with her over the years, starting back in 1996 when I had first

begun reporting on the Elwha dams, then for the *Spokane Spokesman-Review*. I brought her a blanket as a gift, out of respect. By the spring of 2011, she was ninety-three, one of the oldest living members of the tribe and few remaining speakers of the tribe's native language. She and her niece, Bea Charles, had come to embody the power of persistence that finally helped bring about what the tribe had sought for generations.

Smith lived in a simple double-wide, recently repainted in turquoise and yellow. It was May, and a silvery spring rain was falling as we arrived. The dog on a chain across the street from her house had worn a circle of packed earth under the circumference of its life. It was tribal election time, and hand-painted signs were on the telephone poles. In such a small community, no last names were needed. Just: "Re-Elect Raz," or "Vote for Russ."

I found Smith dressed up in red velveteen for Steve's camera. Her faced was deeply lined, her voice soft. She'd had a fall months ago that was bothering one of her arms, and she was still adjusting to the death of her niece, Bea, a few years earlier. Born just a year apart, they were each orphaned before they were out of high school and grew up together with their relatives. They had gone to boarding school together too, then headed off to Seattle together to find jobs, eventually returning to the reservation, where they became deeply committed to reviving the tribe's native language, teaching it not only on the reservation, but also in the Port Angeles high school in one of the first public school native language initiatives in Washington State. Wendy Sampson, Smith's protégée in Klallam instruction, was now certified to teach the language in public schools. She had given Smith a Chihuahua for comfort, and the dog quivered with excitement at our arrival. In the tiny

The Elwha restoration is also a cultural renewal for the tribe. Tribal members saw the prayers of generations of their elders answered in a ceremony celebrating the beginning of dam removal held above Elwha Dam in September, 2011.

As Elwha Dam came out in March, 2012 and Lake Aldwell drained, floodwaters receded exposing not only the river's native channel, pictured here, but the tribe's sacred creation site, rediscovered after one hundred years.

space with the tiny dog—named Kiwi, and just as round and fat as its namesake fruit—we suddenly felt very big.

I tucked myself next to Adeline on the couch and we settled in for a talk with the steady rain drumming in the background. Born in 1918, between completion of the two dams in 1914 and 1927, Smith had outlived three children and two husbands. Over the course of her life she had welded submarines, worked as a riveter at Boeing, eviscerated chickens at a meatpacking plant, sewn jackets at a Seattle garment factory, worked at the Goodwill store on Dearborn Avenue in Seattle,

and picked salal in the woods for seventeen cents a bunch. As a child, her father told her about Thunderbird's Cave—the place where a rainbow jumped back and forth in the river's mist as it crashed through a tight canyon, and about the tribe's creation site by the Elwha, where the Creator bathed and blessed the Klallam people, and tribal members sought to discern their future.

As a kid she used to sit with Bea by the river on her family's homestead, with the whole family gathered by the smokehouse to watch the fish go upriver on summer evenings. "It was my dad and mother's first house when they first got married, right by the river," Smith said. "When everybody got through with supper, if it was a nice day they would go down to the river and watch the fish go by. You couldn't cross a stream without stepping on a fish, they were that thick; they were so thick, Bea's little brother used to pick them up by the tail. We used to hear them flipping around when they were jumping. They were taller than I was. It was nothing to get a fifty-five pounder. Oh, it just makes my mouth water to think of all the good fish we used to have."

She had seen so much change in her life. Her grandfather Joe Sampson used to run a ferry scow on cables pulled by horses to cross the Elwha for twenty-five cents a ride. And from being punished in school for speaking her native language, today she was sought out as an instructor and had just helped finish her tribe's first written dictionary. But the dams coming out? "I never thought I would see the day," Smith said.

. . .

September 17, 2011, broke clear and beautiful in Port Angeles. Smith turned out for what she and so many others had awaited for so long: to see the first chunks taken out of the Elwha Dam. The invitation-only ceremony gathered tribal members, dignitaries, agency leaders and staff, and some of the activists who had been in the fight the longest. Smith arrived in a wheelchair, with Sampson pushing her along. From an archway fitted over the walkway across the top of the dam, colorful banners commissioned especially for the day created a magical entryway to the gathering grounds. Each was different: A salmon. A bear chowing down on a salmon feast. The words "Welcome Home," and "Elwha Be Free."

Raymond Moses, a tribal fisheries technician, releases one of ten king salmon relocated above the dams for a tracking study. He said he felt "a sigh of relief. Like they were meant to be up here in a part of the watershed they have missed for one hundred years."

Sampson pushed Smith along under the fluttering banners, to the opposite bank of the river. She settled in with a large contingent of tribal members from Lower Elwha, turned out in red and black ceremonial regalia, including handwoven cedar hats decorated with family heirlooms: Ermine tails. Eagle feathers. Both of Washington's US senators, US Representative Norm Dicks, and the Secretary of the Interior, the Commissioner of the Bureau of Reclamation, the governor of Washington, and

Renewal of the Elwha ecosystem will be a long-term process that will outlast our lifetimes. Here the first grasses begin to take hold in the bottom of former Lake Aldwell.

the chairwoman of the Lower Elwha Klallam Tribe shared a stage built just above the river.

Ben Charles Sr., who had blessed the First Salmon ceremony just the month before, offered a prayer to open the commemoration. "There is a lot of positive power here," Charles said as the crowd, seated in rows of plastic folding chairs, quieted. "Prayers are answered today that all down through the years have gone up from my aunties, my uncles, my ancestors. They lived on these waters and prayed when they saw the damages done. When all the things started to happen, many tears were shed. Many lives were lost. But I can see them because they are standing here now, in a great cloud of witness, and they are all so happy, some of them are crying. They are the ones that prayed in earnest, and so many times it seemed prayers were in vain, so many things they were hoping for seemed to fly away. One hundred years. That is a long time to us. But for the Creator, it's just a snap, a blink of an eye. I look at our elders, and to see this, our prayers are answered. Even though so many times we wept, we prayed, we wept some more, some of us had even given up and said, 'What is the use?' And the Creator says, 'Come on. You are just about there.' Every day I pray for courage, for strength, for backbone. Such a beautiful day. Such a great cloud of witnesses, these loved ones who are just watching. It is a time some may have looked forward to, so many prayers directed to, so many actions directed to, and today, we see a beginning. Thank you for so many who worked for this; bless our time of fellowship today, our time of rejoicing. And for those who don't like this, I ask, put them in your hand, know that we love them."

And then finally there came what everyone had been waiting for: the yell from US Secretary of the Interior Ken Salazar,

Worn by time and floodwaters, this bit of tree root was exposed by the river unleashed as Elwha Dam came down. The second dam will be gone by spring of 2013, initiating another cascade of changes in the Elwha.

joined by many in the crowd, to the operator of an excavator down below on the riverbanks, to begin demolition. The operator started up the excavator with a roar, raising and swinging its gold-spray-painted bucket and bringing it down with a smash on the cofferdam that helped hold the Elwha Dam in place for a century. In the audience, Lower Elwha Klallam tribal members rose to their feet and began to beat their drums and sing. On many faces, tears flowed as their song was punctuated with the bash of the excavator on the concrete. "I'm just so happy," said Jamie Valadez, language instructor for the tribe. "An injustice was done a hundred years ago. And now here is a chance to heal not only the fish, but the whole watershed and the people."

After the ceremony, Sampson rolled Smith in her wheelchair back over the dam. Seeing them leave, I ran after them. There was something I wanted to make sure Adeline saw on the way out, on this of all days. I caught up with them just as they were reaching the walkway across the dam. I walked with them to the other side, then asked them to turn and look down. There, directly down below the dam, was the pool. And in it, clearly visible, as if there for the ceremony, were the big chinook, faithfully returned once more for their fall run.

They were circling in the pool at the base of the dam, the same pool so many of their descendants had come back to for so many years—watched, as they stopped there in that pool, by so many generations of this tribe. But theirs would be the last generations to confront this dam. Seeing the fish, Smith's face bloomed with a smile. Then she turned and looked over her shoulder, back at the Elwha, green and sparkling above the dam. She caught my eye, beaming with excitement. "There," she said, pointing upstream. "They are going to go up there."

EPILOGUE

Some of those most involved in the Elwha dams saga have already moved on. Kevin Yancy is still in Port Angeles, now working for Bonneville Power Administration. Operator Billy Cargo now works at Grand Coulee Dam in Eastern Washington. As for the beautiful period equipment in the powerhouses of the Elwha dams, some items were preserved, but the grandest—such as the control panel at the Elwha Dam—were deemed too big and heavy to deal with and were destroyed in place during demolition.

Shawn Cantrell, formerly of Friends of the Earth, still works as executive director of Seattle Audubon, and Brian Winter will retire in a few years from the Park Service. Mel and Sonny Sampson at Lower Elwha are still working for the tribal fisheries program. Adeline Smith just celebrated her ninety-fourth birthday, and all of the scientists we went out with on our forays are still at it, planning follow-up work in the Elwha. Norm Dicks retired in 2012, after serving eighteen terms in Congress. Lake Mills was no more by November, and coho were headed back to the river, finding refuge in clear water side channels as the first big slugs of sediment started coming out from behind what was left of Glines Canyon Dam.

Tim Randle and Jennifer Bountry revisited the Elwha in November, 2012, and discovered even more sediment in the former reservoirs than originally estimated.

Rick Rutz still sticks his head into environmental causes—necessary work, he notes, for every citizen. "The fact is, things like the Elwha, big new things in the interest of the environment, don't get started by agencies or the political process," Rutz said. "They are not miracles that happen out of nowhere, and they are not done because they are a grand, bold experiment.

"They are done because people work hard and ask hard questions and refuse to be put off. They are done because the public makes it happen."

162   Tiny Douglas fir transplants make a bold start. How the renewal of the Elwha ecosystem unfolds after dam removal will be one of the great ecological stories of our lifetime.

RESOURCES

There are a wealth of resources available to learn more about the Elwha restoration, get tips on seeing the restoration for yourself, and find out how to volunteer in the effort.

WEBSITES

Elwha Watershed Information Resource: A rich, well compiled web portal for Elwha research resources, from maps to interviews to reports.
www.elwhainfo.org/

Lower Elwha Klallam Tribe: Features dam removal information and history from the tribe.
www.elwha.org/damremoval.html

National Park Service: Focuses on the Elwha restoration, including links to reports, research, blogs, and webcams. A highly useful one-stop source and ideal for students.
www.nps.gov/olym/naturescience/elwha-ecosystem
-restoration.htm

Also on the National Park service website, you will find information about volunteer opportunities in revegetation of the watershed, and a closer look at the revegetation plan.
www.nps.gov/olym/naturescience/elwha-revegetation.htm

Peninsula College Library: A rich and rewarding selected bibliography about the Elwha River dam removal.
http://pc-library.blogspot.com/2007/10/library-publishes
-elwha-river-dam.html

The Seattle Times: Special report on the Elwha restoration.
www.seattletimes.com/flatpages/specialreports/elwha
/?spotlightname=elwha&spotlightquery=elwha

BOOKS

History

Brown, Bruce. *Mountain in the Clouds: A Search for Wild Salmon*, Seattle: University of Washington Press, 1995.

Crane, Jeff. *Finding the River: An Environmental History of the Elwha*, Corvallis, OR: Oregon State University Press, 2011.

Fish, Harriet U. *The Elwha: A River of Destiny*. Published by the author, out of print, but available in libraries and from quality booksellers.

Lien, Carsten. *Exploring the Olympic Mountains: Accounts of the Earliest Expeditions, 1878–1890*, Seattle: The Mountaineers Books, 2001.

Mapes, Lynda V. *Breaking Ground: The Lower Elwha Klallam Tribe and the Unearthing of Tse-whit-zen Village*, Seattle: University of Washington Press, 2009.

Olympic Peninsula Intertribal Cultural Advisory Committee. *Native Peoples of the Olympic Peninsula: Who We Are.* Edited by Jacilee Wray. Norman, OK: University of Oklahoma Press, 2002.

Wilkinson, Charles. *Messages from Frank's Landing: A Story of Salmon, Treaties, and the Indian Way*, Seattle: University of Washington Press, 2000

Wood, Robert L. *Across the Olympic Mountains: The Press Expedition*, 2nd ed. Seattle: The Mountaineers Books, 1989.

---*The Land that Slept Late: The Olympic Mountains in Legend and History*, Seattle: The Mountaineers Books, 1995.

---*Men, Mules and Mountains: Lieutenant O'Neil's Olympic Expeditions*, Seattle: The Mountaineers Books, 1977.

Natural History and Science

Duda, Jeffrey, Jonathan A. Warrick, and Christopher S. Magirl, eds. *Coastal Habitats of the Elwha River, Washington: Biological and Physical Patterns and Processes Prior to Dam Removal*, Scientific Investigations Report 2011–5120, US Department of the Interior, US Geological Survey. Available for free download online: http://pubs.usgs.gov/sir/2011/5120/

McNulty, Tim. *Olympic National Park: A Natural History*, Seattle: University of Washington Press, 2009.

Northwest Scientific Association. "Dam Removal and Ecosystem Restoration in the Elwha River of Washington State." *Northwest Science, Vol. 82, Special Issue* (2008). Available in libraries or for online purchase at www.bioone.org/toc/nwsc/82/sp1

Peck, Mary. *Away Out Over Everything*, Palo Alto, CA: Stanford University Press, 2004.

RESEARCH VENUES

For the reader seeking to do primary research I would suggest visits to the Clallam County Historical Society (www.clallamhistoricalsociety.com/)in Port Angeles and the Special Collections of the University of Washington Libraries in Seattle (www.lib.washington.edu/specialcollections/) and Washington State Archives in Olympia (www.sos.wa.gov/archives/) where exhaustive troves of historic photographs, correspondence, government reports, newspaper clippings, books, and microfilmed manuscripts could inform virtually any aspect of inquiry on the Elwha, its history and restoration.

CURRENT NEWS REPORTS

Read my stories in *The Seattle Times*, where I am continuing beat coverage of the Elwha restoration, as well as my blog posts in Field Notes, the *Seattle Times* nature blog:

http://seattletimes.com/html/fieldnotes/

All stories on the Elwha are easily accessed without charge online at http://seattletimes.com/html/home/index.html. Type "Elwha" in the search bar and every story or blog post written on the topic published by *The Seattle Times* in print and online will be listed for reading and download. The newspaper's entire digital news archive resides online in perpetuity, and dates back to 1985. The digital photo archive goes back even further.

VISITING THE ELWHA

I urge you to go see the changing landscape of the Elwha for yourself. For tips on where to go and what to see, read "Elwha: See It for Yourself" in Field Notes: http://seattletimes.com/html/fieldnotes/2018188707_see_it_for_yourself_exploring_the_elwha.html

The Elwha revegetation and fish restoration plans are intended to respond to changing conditions as the restoration progresses. Weeds such as this flower in the former Elwha lake beds are no problem, but invasive reed canary grass prompted early intervention with herbicide.

Brave new shoots make a start in the former Lake Aldwell. Revegetation of the inhospitable lakebed was off to a stronger start than expected after removal of Elwha Dam, with growth of alders reaching head high.

INDEX

Lynda Mapes and Steve Ringman of *The Seattle Times* teamed up to tell the story of the largest dam removal ever. Glines Canyon Dam was still intact as Steve one-handed this shot taken in spring, 2011.

ABOUT THE AUTHOR

Lynda V. Mapes is a reporter at *The Seattle Times*, where she specializes in coverage of Native American tribes, nature, and environmental topics. Lynda has received many national and regional awards for her work. Along with her teammates on the Elwha coverage at *The Seattle Times*, she shared the 2012 award for online journalism from the American Association for the Advancement of Science. Her previous books are *Breaking Ground* (University of Washington Press, 2009) about the inadvertent discovery of an ancient Indian village on the Port Angeles waterfront during a state construction project, and *Washington, the Spirit of the Land* (Voyageur Press, 1999) a large format photography book about the landscapes of Washington State. A native of New York and 1981 graduate of Oberlin College, she moved to the Pacific Northwest in 1992 after working as a political reporter for two newspapers in Maryland. She joined the staff of *The Seattle Times* in 1997. An active hiker, birder, and gardener, she lives with her husband, Douglas B. MacDonald, in the Greenwood neighborhood of Seattle.

ABOUT THE PHOTOGRAPHER

Steve Ringman is a general assignment photographer for *The Seattle Times*. He shoots everything from sports to features but his passion and personal focus is on stories involving environmental issues including climate change, fisheries, and forestry.
A native of Washington State, Ringman first worked for the *San Francisco Chronicle* where he teamed with Randy Shilts for a year documenting the first extensive newspaper coverage of people with AIDS. He covered major stories including the Sandinista–Contra war, aging in America, and the blight of indigent hotels and their residents in San Francisco's Tenderloin District.

Based in Seattle since 1992, Ringman has traveled to the Arctic covering climate change and to Africa covering the efforts to eradicate malaria. Steve has developed and honed his multimedia skills shooting video along with stills to engage and inform readers, enabling readers to walk with him and visualize stories such as the plight of the troubled Puget Sound abalone, and the devastation of the bark beetle outbreak in Washington's Methow Valley.

A graduate of Brooks Institute of Photography, Ringman was twice named national Newspaper Photographer of the Year by the National Press Photographers Association. Most recently he was a co-winner of the 2009 Knight Foundation's Risser Award for Environmental Reporting with coverage on landslides caused by over-logging and the environmental damage that followed. He currently lives in Seattle with his wife, Evelyn.

ABOUT THE SEATTLE TIMES

The Seattle Times is the trusted source for Northwest news, information, and entertainment for people who care about thoughtful, independent journalism. Founded in 1896 by Alden J. Blethen, *The Seattle Times* is a fourth- and fifth-generation family business and one of the few remaining family-owned and independent metropolitan newspapers in the United States.

The history of The Seattle Times Company is rooted in the principles of independence, family ownership, journalistic excellence and community service. A nine-time winner of the coveted Pulitzer Prize, *The Seattle Times* is known for outstanding journalism and is the second-largest newspaper on the West Coast. Its website, seattletimes.com, is the largest local news and information site in the Northwest. Committed to delivering news and information via platforms widely embraced by consumers, *The Times* is available on multiple formats including print, website, digital replica, smartphone, and tablet apps.

Other Blethen-owned newspapers in Washington are the *Walla Walla Union-Bulletin*, the *Yakima Herald-Republic*, *The Issaquah Press*, the *Newcastle News*, the *Sammamish Review*, and the *SnoValley Star*.

seattletimes.com

THE MOUNTAINEERS, founded in 1906, is a nonprofit outdoor activity and conservation organization whose mission is "to explore, study, preserve, and enjoy the natural beauty of the outdoors…." Based in Seattle, Washington, it is now one of the largest such organizations in the United States, with seven branches throughout Washington State.

The Mountaineers sponsors both classes and year-round outdoor activities in the Pacific Northwest, which include hiking, mountain climbing, ski-touring, snowshoeing, bicycling, camping, canoeing and kayaking, nature study, sailing, and adventure travel. The Mountaineers' conservation division supports environmental causes through educational activities, sponsoring legislation, and presenting informational programs.

All activities are led by skilled, experienced volunteers, who are dedicated to promoting safe and responsible enjoyment and preservation of the outdoors.

If you would like to participate in these organized outdoor activities or programs, consider a membership in The Mountaineers. For information and an application, write or call the Mountaineers Program Center, 7700 Sand Point Way NE, Seattle, WA 98115-3996; phone 206-521-6001; visit www.mountaineers.org; or email info@mountaineers.org.

The Mountaineers Books, an active, nonprofit publishing program of The Mountaineers, produces guidebooks, instructional texts, historical works, natural history guides, and works on environmental conservation. All books produced by The Mountaineers Books fulfill the mission of The Mountaineers. Visit www.mountaineersbooks.org to find details about all our titles and the latest author events, as well as videos, web clips, links, and more!

The Mountaineers Books
1001 SW Klickitat Way, Suite 201
Seattle, WA 98134
800-553-4453
mbooks@mountaineersbooks.org